DISGUSTING
FACTS

DISGUSTING FACTS

by

Martyn Hamer

This is a Parragon Book
First published in 2000

Parragon
Queen Street House
4 Queen Street
Bath BA1 1HE, UK

Produced by Magpie Books, an imprint of
Constable Robinson Ltd, London

ISBN 0-75253-524-2 (Hardback)
ISBN 0-75253-947-7 (Paperback)

A copy of the British Library Cataloguing-in-Publication Data
is available from the British Library

Printed and bound in Indonesia

CONTENTS

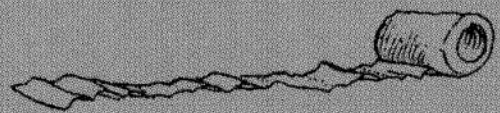

CHAPTER ONE

It's An Ill Wind

We all do it. Ordinary people, famous people, royalty – we all do it. What is it? Passing wind is what we're on about, something not discussed in polite company, but laughed about with friends. For some strange reason it is embarrassing to let out a loud fart when other people are around, which should not really be the case because it is a perfectly natural function – although it can often be quite smelly.

Read the following fart facts and you will soon become an expert on something that most adults will not let you talk about!

What Is A Fart?

Farting and, incidentally, belching is simply your body's way of getting rid of some of the air that you swallowed while eating and gases that result from the chemical processes of digestion.

Wind can also be caused by certain foods. It can also be brought on by gulping in too much air when eating, eating too fast, or even by just slouching in a chair.

Beanz Meanz Farts

A particular brand of baked beans used to be advertised with a little ditty which finished with the line "Beanz meanz Heinz". It did not take long for the wits to make it into this witty ditty:

A million housewives every day
Pick up a tin of beans and say
Beanz meanz farts.

Great Wind Makers

Beans are in fact great wind makers. This is because they contain two sugars, raffinose and stacchyose. Our stomach enzymes deal with most sugars very efficiently but these two are tougher to process. As a result they remain in the gut and bacteria start feeding on them. The sugars ferment in the bacteria and gas is produced. There is only one good way of getting rid of this excess gas. That's it – a good loud trumpet!

Cut It Out

If you like beans but do not want to fart (well, not much), the beans should be soaked thoroughly and pre-cooked. It is reckoned that this can cut down the wind by up to 60 per cent. We are not talking about tinned beans here: if you pre-soak them you just make the tins go rusty!

It's A Gas!

Most of the gas in a fart, 99 per cent in fact, is composed of hydrogen and carbon dioxide, which do not smell. But here comes the bad news: the remaining 1 per cent consists of hydrogen sulphide and other smelly things, which do tend to whiff a bit!

Wind Power

The German reformer, theologian and writer Martin Luther, who lived from 1483 to 1546, suffered greatly with constipation and boasted that he could "drive away the evil spirit with a single fart".

A Cure That Takes The Biscuit

Digestive biscuits were originally invented as a means of cutting down excessive wind.

Fart Dampers

Japanese ladies often take a small torch-like device with them when they go into a public toilet. This makes the noise of a flushing toilet and drowns out any loud farts or other natural sounds that the ladies may make. Some modern toilets have wall-mounted devices that provide the same covering noise.

Lord Of The Wind

When the Earl of Oxford bowed to Queen Elizabeth I he trumped accidentally. He was so concerned about it that he left Britain for seven years. When he returned to court, thinking the queen would have forgotten about his misdemeanour, the queen greeted him with, "Hallo, you old fart".

Beethoven's Fart Symphony

Rajiv Kamir, a train announcer in Madras, India, was sacked from his job in September 1996. He had played Beethoven's Fifth Symphony over the public address system. With luck he might have got away with that but his bosses disapproved of the way he farted in tune with the music, which was heard by all the travellers on the station.

Perhaps Beethoven's Fifth Symphony should now be renamed Beethoven's Fart Symphony?

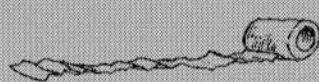

Wind Instrumentalist

A rather loud and smelly fart also led to the sacking of an oboist with the Kansas City Symphony Orchestra in 1993. He had been reprimanded after a complaint about him and his response was the release of an appropriate amount of wind during a rehearsal of the *Nutcracker* – a response that was not appreciated by general manager Susan Franano.

What A Smelly Job!

In the mid to late eighteenth century a slang term for a footman or valet was "fart-catcher" because he had to walk behind his master.

Health Hazard

Working in an office with colleagues who fart can damage your health, according to Swedish scientists. It is reckoned that high levels of human gas can cause serious health problems to those who inhale it.

Famous Farters

Queen Victoria

In the British court Queen Victoria was quite famous for her passing of wind, produced mainly by the fact that she ate too quickly.

Next time you get told off for farting say you are doing an impression of Queen Victoria.

King Louis

King Louis XIV of France was a great French farter (no connection with a frankfurter, which is something entirely different). When he let off a

loud trumpet in the presence of his sister-in-law, the Duchess of Orleans, he said it was a sign of his admiration for her.

Hitler

The German leader Adolf Hitler had quite a problem with farting. His personal doctor, Dr Theodore Morell, treated the Führer with Dr

Köster's Anti-Gas Pills. As these contained the poisons belladonna and strychnine they probably did the patient more harm than good.

The Art Of Fart

Le Pétomane

A French baker, Joseph Pujol, who was born in Marseilles on 1 June 1857, was famous for his expertise at passing wind. Under the stage name of Le Pétomane (The Crazy Farter) he appeared in theatres demonstrating his unique skills. Just by passing wind he could do imitations of various sounds and even play tunes! Among his imitations he included the sound of a dressmaker tearing cloth – a tremendous fart that lasted ten seconds – a cannon, and the noise of thunder. One of his specialities was to blow out a candle from 30 cm (12 inches) away just by bending over and

blowing off. He continued to perform until the outbreak of the First World War, when he returned to baking.

Incidentally, Le Pétomane's wind performances were odourless – just as well, or the audience would have had to wear gas masks to watch him.

La Mère Alexandre

A lady known as La Mère Alexandre did a similar act to Le Pétomane. La Mére Alexandre was also a bit of an impressionist, for one of the highlights of her act was "farts of the famous". She also did impressions of how people in different professions farted.

Jingle Farts

A rendering of *Jingle Bells* on the anal wind instrument was one of the specialities of a lady called Honeysuckle Divine who performed in America in the 1980s. A handy lady to have around at Christmas – provided that she didn't blow out all the Christmas candles at the same time.

Even Animals Do It!

Macho Gas

Lord Lucan, an English aristocrat who disappeared in mysterious circumstances in 1974, had a Dobermann Pinscher dog. Lucan allowed the dog to sleep on his bed because he liked to hear it fart. He said it was a very masculine thing.

Farting Sheep

Scientists believe that too much farting can affect global warming. Scientists in New Zealand are studying the farting and belching habits of sheep. They have fitted the animals with measuring devices on their bums and mouths to monitor the effects. We hear a lot about the effects of carbon dioxide on global warming but apparently farting is even more responsible. Indeed it has been suggested that this is a possible cause of the disappearance of the dinosaurs. They gassed themselves to

death! So, if you want to be environmentally friendly, stop farting.

Could Cow Burps Be Used As Fuel?

This was a question investigated by scientists in Fort Worth, Texas, a few years ago. They worked out that if bovine burps could be recycled, the gas from just ten cows could keep a small house heated for a year. They would probably have got better results if they had concentrated on the other end of the cow. Ask your mum for a herd of cows for your birthday and you could cut down on your fuel bills.

CHAPTER TWO

Medical Mayhem

In days gone by, when there were none of the modern medical facilities we enjoy today, people relied upon many weird and wonderful remedies to cure their ills. Whether any of them worked is another matter.

Don't Try These At Home . . .

Sheep droppings boiled in milk were once recommended in Ireland as a cure for whooping cough. Another supposed cure was a spoonful of woodlice, bruised and mixed with breast milk.

In the seventeenth century a cure for chapped lips was to take sweat from behind your ears and rub it on your mouth.

A much recommended medicine for all ills in Elizabethan times was powdered human skull dissolved in red wine. It is not recorded if the drink had a head on it.

A popular cure for a cough used to be snails boiled in barley water. Most people would probably rather have had the cough.

Doctors once used leeches as a cure for many ills. The leeches sucked blood from the patient and this was thought to be a good thing. Strangely enough, some modern doctors are now using the same technique.

When In Rome . . .

The chariot racers of ancient Rome had an unusual method of developing their muscles. They used a drink made from dried boar's dung. The gladiators were probably not that strong – they just smelled that way.

In ancient Rome it was also believed that drinking fresh gladiator's blood was a cure for epilepsy. People used to wait at the exits from gladiatorial arenas to collect the blood as the dead gladiators were dragged out.

Ways With Wee

A red rag soaked in urine and salt and tied around the wrist was once said to cure a sprain.

Fancy a mouthwash? If you do, don't try the methods of the ancient Romans. They made mouthwash and toothpaste with urine.

Fresh urine contains no bacteria so it has

been used as an antiseptic, to bathe wounds, when there was no antiseptic to hand.

Wart A Way To Go

There are many folk remedies for warts, some more disgusting than others. One method was to rub a piece of stolen meat on the wart and then bury it. The belief was that as the meat rotted the wart would fade away.

The blood of moles was once used to cure warts. (Did the patient then develop moles?)

You Need This Like A Hole In The Head

For thousands of years it was believed that *trepanning* – drilling a hole in the skull – was a cure for many ailments because the hole allowed evil spirits to escape. A large number of

ancient skulls have been found with primitive holes bored in them and, quite amazingly, many people seem to have survived this frightening operation. How boring!

A Head For Headaches

One ancient way to relieve headaches was to swallow some powdered human skull. Sounds bad enough to give you a headache just thinking about it.

Website Cures

Many people still believe that putting a spider's web on a wound will staunch the bleeding. It is thought that the blood will stick to the strands of the web and this will help a clot and a subsequent scab to form more easily. But if you tried it *you* would be the clot, because spider's webs carry dirt and other matter that could well cause an infection.

At one time swallowing whole spiders and their webs was considered to be a cure for jaundice.

Spiders rolled in butter was regarded as a

cure for malaria in the seventeenth century. Eating buttered live spiders was also once a recommended cure for a headache.

Hee-Haw Healing

An old German cure for toothache was to kiss a donkey.

A donkey also formed part of a cure for whooping cough. In Yorkshire, England, it was believed that the hairs from a donkey's back eaten on bread and butter would cure the ailment.

In 1827, the British painter John Constable was concerned about the health of his young son, who was suffering with whooping cough. He was advised to pass the boy three times over and three times under a donkey.

Ideas For Influenza

An old American folk remedy for influenza was a strip of raw pork wrapped around your neck with a salted herring attached to it (a sort of herring aid!).

Another "remedy" was to bandage your chest with cabbage leaves, replacing them when they became transparent.

Both of these cures were probably very smelly indeed.

Fast Operators

Even as late as the mid-nineteenth century the conditions in hospital operating theatres were rather primitive. Because of this, the key to effective amputations was speed. The surgeon Robert Liston held the record, being able to amputate a leg in just twenty-five seconds.

But frequently the speed of the operation was of no help. The complete lack of any form of antiseptic nearly always resulted in the patient's wound getting infected, and death often followed.

Coat Of Many Colours

A bloody coat was once considered to be the sign of a good surgeon. The more senior the surgeon, the bloodier the coat. Sawdust was scattered on the floors of hospital operating theatres to soak up the blood from amputations, which were performed without the aid of any form of anaesthetic. The smell of the theatre was often so bad that medical students watching had to smoke to cover up the stench.

Forceps, Please!

In 1970 a man had an operation to remove a pair of hospital forceps that had been discovered in his body. He had fallen downstairs and, because he complained of pain in his ribcage, was given an X-ray. This showed a metal object to the left above the diaphragm and a subsequent operation brought forth the forceps. They were rusting at the hinge, which was hardly surprising since it was revealed that they had been there ever since an operation performed sixteen years previously.

Botched Job

Not all surgery is as successful as one would hope. Robert Liston, the ninteenth-century surgeon mentioned earlier, once amputated three fingers of an assistant's hand. The only problem was that the assistant was not the patient and that the patient had attended the hospital to have a leg amputated. He may have been fast but it sounds as if he was not very accurate!

Hole In One

Back in the nineteenth century a French-Canadian trapper, Alexis St Martin, proved to be a great help to the modern understanding of the human digestive system. His stomach had been shot away in a shooting accident, leaving him with a gaping hole in his body. An American army doctor, William Beaumont, used this hole in

experiments to watch the passage of food and drink through the body. He even tied pieces of food on lengths of string, lowered them into the open stomach and withdrew them at intervals to see how digestion was progressing.

This may sound disgusting but the work was

to prove extremely valuable. In fact Beaumont made 238 tests on St Martin and wrote a book based on his case, called *Experiments And Observations On The Gastric Juices And The Physiology Of Digestion*. This was published in 1833.

Oiling Wounds

The recommended treatment for gunshot wounds incurred during battles in the sixteenth century was to pour boiling oil over them. It was believed that the wounds were poisonous and the oil would counteract this. It no doubt resulted in the patient enduring more pain than if the wound had been completely ignored.

Gin Tonic

When Field Marshal Gebhard von Blücher was thrown off his horse at the Battle of Waterloo he was massaged with a mixture of gin and onions. He then remounted and helped the Duke of Wellington win the battle against the French. Perhaps the smell of the booze and the onions kept the enemy at bay.

African Ant-ics

Some strange things have been used to heal wounds but one of the weirdest must be the method used by some tribes in Africa. The soldier ant has powerful pincers and once it has got a grip on something it never lets go. Even if its body gets broken away from the head the ant retains its grip. This ability is used to stitch up a wound. An ant is placed on the cut until it digs its pincers into the flesh. Then the body is broken off, leaving just the head to hold the wound together until it heals.

Post-Operative Pigeon

According to the second-century Greek physician Galen, open wounds after an operation should be treated with the blood of pigeons. Galen's works formed the basis of medical teaching for over a thousand years and probably resulted in the deaths of millions of people because many of his ideas about how the body works were completely wrong.

Plague Tales

Don't Blame The Rats

Rats are often blamed for the bubonic plague that rampaged through Europe in the seventeenth century. In fact the main culprits were the fleas that lived on the infected rats. On biting an infected rat, the flea would suck up the single-celled bacillus that caused the plague. These bacilli congregated inside the flea and clogged its stomach valve. This caused the flea to go on a feeding spree which, if it led to it biting a human, would mean that the poor person got a dose of the plague.

Birdbrained Idea
During the French plague of 1720, doctors in Marseilles wore a special mask to protect themselves. It looked like a bird's head and the beak was filled with spices to purify the air being breathed. Needless to say, it did not do any good.

And A "Cure" . . .
Washing the patient in goat's urine was one of the recommended cures for the bubonic plague. Yuck!

Drugs From A To B
The scientist Sir Francis Galbon once started an experiment with the effects of drugs. He planned to test them on himself in alphabetical order. However, he abandoned the experiment at letter C when he realized that a large dose of

castor oil would prove to be a very powerful laxative.

Deadly Dyspepsia

Many people take powders to relieve indigestion but it did not do Susan Lowder of Burlington, Massachusetts, any good. Her gravestone reads:

Here lies the body of Susan Lowder
Who burst while drinking Seidlitz powder
Called from this world to her heavenly rest
She should have waited till it effervesced

Bad Physicians

In the Middle Ages a contest was held between two doctors at the royal court of Salerno, Italy, to see which of them had the greater knowledge of drugs. The first man to poison the other was declared the winner.

Scurvy Sailors

Teething Troubles

Up until the eighteenth century more sailors died from disease than from enemy action. One of the most prevalent diseases was *scurvy*, which affected the limbs and joints. Sufferers also had sore gums, loose teeth, skin rashes and bruises.

The first symptoms of scurvy are skin rashes and bruising, followed by the sore gums which eventually become so bad that the teeth fall out. Internal bleeding causes the back and joints to become very painful, old wounds open up and new wounds don't heal. Other than that you feel fine!

A Fruity Cure

The great English navigator Captain James Cook was the first person to try to find a cure for scurvy. He noticed that many of the symptoms disappeared when a ship was in port because the crew were able to get fresh fruit and vegetables. During his voyages of exploration, he put in to as many ports as possible to ensure a regular supply of fresh fruit and vegetables. As a result, his men remained relatively free of the disease.

In 1812 a British naval surgeon discovered that a regular supply of lime juice prevented scurvy and made sure that British sailors were given a regular ration. This led to British sailors being nicknamed "limeys", a name Americans still give the British to this day.

Vitamins Are Vital

In Captain Cook's day it was thought that scurvy was caused by poisons in the food but it was later discovered that the cause was a lack of vitamin C. It is reckoned that for good health we need some 6,500 units of vitamins a day. It is possible to buy vitamin pills but these are not normally necessary if you have good varied meals, which will provide you with all the vitamins you need.

The Disease That Founded A Nation

In 1650 the Dutch East India Company decided to create a refreshment station on the Cape of Good Hope. The idea was to grow fresh fruit and vegetables for the crews of their ships to avoid outbreaks of scurvy on the long voyages from Europe to the East Indies.

The settlement was put under the control of a ship's doctor, Jan van Riebeeck, who arrived with his men on 6 April 1652. A permanent colony was formed and governed by van Riebeeck for ten years, laying the foundations for what is now the city of Cape Town and the country of South Africa.

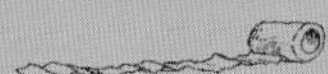

Does Mummy Know Best? – Part One

A popular fifteenth-century cure for bone fractures, paralysis, tuberculosis and other ills was ground-up Egyptian mummies. Eventually Egypt banned the export of mummies so some unscrupulous traders made fake mummies with the bodies of people who themselves had probably died from infectious diseases.

Not everyone praised mummy powder. One doctor said it caused "paine of the heart or stomake, vomiting, and stinke of the mouth". Hardly surprising when you think about it. And it proves that mummy doesn't always know best. Eating live slugs used to be regarded as an excellent cure for tuberculosis. Makes a change from mummy powder anyway.

In some parts of America it was the practice as late as the 1920s to eat live snails as a cure for tuberculosis.

Mum's The Word

Our word "mummy" for an embalmed, bandaged body comes from the Persian word "mum", meaning "wax".

Does Mummy Know Best? – Part Two

A cholera epidemic in the American state of Maine was caused by Egyptian mummies. A man named Augustus Stanwood came up with the bizarre idea that the bandages from mummies could be used to make paper. Unfortunately the bandages were so old and stained that they could not be used to make writing paper, so Stanwood made them into brown paper instead, which he sold to butchers and grocers for wrapping food. No wonder people fell ill.

Fearsome Phobias

If you suffer from nelophobia you have a fear of glass. What a pane.

If you suffer from dystychiphobia you have a fear of accidents.

If you suffer from hodophobia you have a fear of travel.

If you suffer from pognophobia you have a fear of beards.

If you suffer from trichophobia you have a fear of hair.

If you suffer from kyphobia you have a fear of stooping.

If you suffer from alliumphobia you have a fear of garlic (something Dracula suffered from).

And if you suffer from pantophobia you do not have to worry about the others for it is a fear of everything.

If you are now sick of all these long words perhaps you could be going down with a bout of emetophobia, which is a fear of vomiting.

The Tooth, The Whole Tooth And Nothing But The Tooth

To cure toothache ancient Egyptians would take a live mouse and slit it open. This was then laid over the offending tooth.

The Greek physician Hippocrates, who lived from around 460 to 377 BC and is known as "the father of modern medicine", suggested a toothpaste made from three mice and the head of a hare as a cure for toothache.

Putting a live louse into a tooth cavity was once thought to be a cure for toothache.

The ancient Romans believed that the best way to get rid of toothache was to tie a toad to your jaw.

John Gaddesden, a fourteenth-century English doctor, suggested that rotting teeth could be removed by rubbing them with dried cow's dung.

It was once the fashion to have all one's teeth pulled out. This was done because it was believed that they could poison the rest of the body. (And then all your friends could call you "Gummy".)

Plop Or Plonk?

A new cure for preventing people from drinking too much alcohol became very popular in Taipei, Taiwan, in 1992 – tiger dung! The tiger plop was dried and then ground into a powder which was mixed into a glass of wine. Sounds revolting – enough to put anyone off drinking!

A Worm In Your Ear

In 1997 a man went to his doctor complaining about discomfort in his right ear. When he was examined it was discovered that his ear was full of maggots! It was thought that a fly must have laid some eggs in his ear a few days before when he had fallen asleep on a beach. Doctors filled the ear with castor oil and the maggots floated out.

Saved By Bacon

During a holiday in Belize in 1996 Lee Miller, a private in the British Territorial Army, was bitten on the head by a botfly. The bite injected an egg beneath his skin, which developed into a maggot. Six weeks later, doctors at the Royal Hallamshire Hospital in Sheffield, England, had to draw the maggot out. They did this with rashers of bacon. The patient had his scalp bandaged with bacon for thirty hours. Apparently this starved the maggot of oxygen and it eventually emerged from beneath Lee's skin to have a quick bacon snack!

There's an amazing fact to impress your friends!

Crabby Cure

Crab dung is being used by surgeons to mend broken bones. Mixed with salt water or blood, it hardens and has proved better than either plastic or metal for knitting bones together. This revolutionary technique was discovered by accident when scientists at Reading University, England, were studying the effects of pollution on marine life. Let's hope that patients receiving this treatment do not become crabby or start walking sideways as a result.

Snakes Alive!

Cobra Chow Mein

Wang Biao, a Chinese peasant, suffered with convulsions. He cured himself by eating 1,800 live poisonous snakes over a two-year period. Apparently this strange, and very dangerous, treatment did get rid of the convulsions. It did, however, have one unusual side effect: he became addicted to eating snakes! In 1985 it was announced that he had to have a snake before every meal, and to make sure he had enough to keep him going he had actually started breeding them.

Turkish Delight?

In 1979 a Turkish girl, Yeter Yilderim, was taken to a hospital in Ankara. She had been suffering from severe stomach pains and splitting headaches. When doctors X-rayed the teenager they found the strange cause of these symptoms – three water snakes some five centimetres long living in her stomach. We have all heard of butterflies in the stomach but snakes seems to be taking things a bit too far.

First, Catch Your Worm . . .

Perhaps the doctors in Turkey could have got rid of the snakes using the device invented by Alpheus Myers, a doctor from Indiana, USA, in 1854. His invention was an instrument for extracting tapeworms from a patient. His remarkable invention consisted of a small baited trap attached to a length of string. The patient had to fast for a while to make the tapeworm hungry. Then he swallowed the trap, leaving the string hanging from his mouth. The idea was that the worm would then take the bait, get caught in the trap, and be pulled out of the patient with the string.

Hair Today, Gone Tomorrow

If you know anyone who is going bald you could recommend the Tudor recipe for lessening hair loss – dog or horse pee rubbed into the scalp.

In Panama, Central America, the recommended cure for baldness is a potion made from the bladders of monkeys, tea, and honey. The potion, known as "bladder oil", is also said to cure bad teeth. Obviously a useful thing to have around the house.

Eating rats was considered by the Chinese to be the best way of preventing hair loss.

Cow dung rubbed on to the head will cure baldness according to farmers in Norway.

A remedy for hair loss in ancient Egypt was snake oil and bats' ears.

And while we are on the subject of hair here's another hairy story:

Something To Chew On

A woman in Phoenix, Arizona, had a hair ball removed from her stomach. It was the size of a football. Apparently she had the nervous habit of chewing her hair and it had gradually built up inside her over the years.

Mary Made Them Sick

Typhoid Mary was the nickname given to an American woman, Mary Mallon, who infected over a thousand people with typhoid in the 1900s. In spite of the fact that she knew she was a carrier, she worked, using false names, in several jobs that involved preparing food.

Mary was eventually jailed and she remained in detention right up to her death in 1938. She always proclaimed her innocence but it is known that she was responsible for fifty-three separate outbreaks of the disease.

CHAPTER THREE

Animal Crackers

Come To The Circus

Although most people do not like fleas, flea circuses used to be a popular form of entertainment at fairs right up until the middle of the twentieth century. The fleas would pull tiny carriages, wear tiny dresses in which they danced, and perform duels with miniature swords!

No doubt the owners of such circuses had to start from scratch!

Berlolotto's Flea Circus

One of the most famous flea circuses was that of Signor Berlolotto in London in the 1830s. His show was described in the diary of a lady called Elizabeth Walker in 1833:

"Went to see a curious exhibition of fleas by a M. Berlolotto as follows:

A coach drawn by four fleas, a coachman

and a footman, both fleas, the former shakes his whip.

A ship with masts, sails and cordage, drawn by a single flea – it was, the man said, 120 times its own weight.

An elephant with a tower on its back drawn by a flea.

A ballroom in which two fleas waltz, the musicians are all fleas, they are twelve in

number; these are all on a musical box and when that plays the instruments all move.

The Duke of Wellington and the Bey of Algiers each mounted on a flea.

Two fleas decide an affair of honour with swords.

A flea pulls a pail out of a well.

These fleas, the man told us, are taught to walk by being put in a circular box for about eight days and their education is finished in six weeks. It certainly is very extraordinary, as also is the making of the very small things to which they are attached."

Flea Fact 1

Christina, Queen of Sweden in the seventeenth century, had a special 12 cm long (5 inches) miniature cannon with which she used to shoot at fleas.

Flea Market

Schoolchildren were enjoying an active trade in fleas in Bulgaria in 1992 until the authorities stepped in to stop it. The fleas were changing hands amongst the pupils because education regulations stated that any pupil with fleas had to take three days off school!

Hopping Horrors

The ancient Greeks believed that fleas could be warded off by shouting, "Ouch! Ouch!"

Flea Fact 2

Fleas always jump backwards and land on their back legs.

Bloodshot Eyes

The horned lizard that lives in the deserts of Mexico has an unusual way of defending itself. It spits blood from its eyes!

When the lizard gets very angry its blood pressure rises so fast that it ruptures a blood vessel behind the eyes. The blood shoots out a considerable distance towards the enemy, which, presumably, does not like the idea of being splattered with blood.

Impolite Society

Queen Henrietta, wife of King Leopold II who ruled Belgium from 1865 to 1909, had a pet llama. She taught it to spit in the face of anyone who stroked it.

Poo Pushers

Scarab beetles eat animal dung. They roll large balls of dung into specially dug holes for themselves and their larvae to eat. These balls of poo are sometimes fifty times the weight of the beetle. That is equivalent to a twelve-stone man pushing a weight of four tons!

Some dung beetles are so sensitive to the smell of dung that they rush towards it before it even hits the ground!

Whiffy Lizards

Most dinosaurs were vegetarians so they must have suffered quite a lot with wind. When they farted it must have sounded like thunder. Perhaps that is why the Brontosaurus is also known as the "thunder lizard"? Maybe others should have been nicknamed belchosaurus or maybe fartosaurus! And the smell must have

been atrocious, like a large pile of rotting cabbage, so perhaps there was also a smellysaurus and a stinkysaurus.

Jobbie Jottings

Pouch Poo

Baby kangaroos spend much of their early life in their mother's pouch and also go to the toilet in there. To keep it clean the mother licks it out. Bet you wouldn't fancy licking out your toilet. Ugh!

Meanwhile In China . . .

Giant pandas poo nearly fifty times a day. Wonder what they do in their spare time?

Spread It About

When hippos poo in a river they wag their tails in it to spread it around as much as possible. It gives every other animal around the chance to have a sniff!

King Pong

Mountain gorillas often eat their own droppings. Makes a change from bananas perhaps?

Desk Dung

Fancy an unusual paperweight? A mail order company called Endangered Feces in Alabama, USA, supplies them made from fossilized dinosaur poo.

Excrement Ornament

In America it is possible to buy garden gnomes made from cow dung.

A Messy Trade

The most important industry in the Pacific island of Nauru is the collection of bird droppings. The bird poo, or *guano* as it is called, is exported to other countries for use as a fertilizer.

Barfing In A Big Way

When toads puke they bring up their stomach as well as the sick inside. The toad wipes the sick from its mouth and then swallows its stomach again.

Friends Don't Like Worms

The first series of the American television situation comedy *Friends* had Marcel the monkey in its cast. But Marcel did not last very long. He was thrown out of the series because of his habit of puking up live worms during filming.

Scurf's Up

When monkeys groom one another they are not looking for fleas as many people think. They are picking out bits of scurf which they then eat.

Human Flypaper

If you want to keep flies out of the kitchen put a bucket of dung in the dining room.

Ancient Egyptians used the same principle by smearing a servant with ass's milk. The poor

unfortunate was then made to stand in a corner of the room to attract the flies.

No Wonder She's A Widow

The black widow spider eats her partner after mating. Often she will get through twenty-five partners a day.

Love Him To Death

The female praying mantis eats her mate while they are mating! She starts at his head and works her way down his body. When she has eaten all of him mating is completed and the father provides useful nourishment for his offspring!

Inside Job

The hagfish, an eel-like creature sometimes called a slime fish, attaches itself to its prey with its sharp teeth. It then curls itself up like a corkscrew and gradually screws itself into the flesh. Eventually it gets right inside the fish and then starts eating it from the inside until just the skin and bones are left.

Beetle Baubles

A popular fashion accessory in Cuba are luminous beetles known as fireflies. When stimulated they glow on and off in the dark. Cuban women attach them to their clothing or around their necks as a form of living jewellery. That's one way of getting bugged.

Scenting Danger

When a skunk is in danger it sprays out a foul-smelling liquid from its anal glands. The smell is so powerful it can be detected up to half a mile away. Strange as it may seem, the same liquid with the pong removed is used for making top perfumes.

Feeding Frenzy

Graveyard Gourmets

Many flies lay their eggs on dead animals. The maggots which hatch from the eggs feed voraciously on the rotting flesh.

Sexton beetles have antennae which are especially sensitive to the smell of dead animals. Soon after a creature dies the beetles home in on it and rush to grab the flesh for their larvae.

They dig beneath the dead creature until it is eventually buried then they lay their eggs on the carcass. When the baby beetles hatch they are ensured of a hearty meal on the decaying flesh.

What A Food Chain!

The ichneumon wasp of North America lays its eggs in the pupa of the tachnid fly and the tachnid fly lays its eggs in the larva of the Mexican bean beetle!

Toad In A Hole

There is a horsefly larva in North America that feeds on young toads. The larva buries itself in the mud of ponds and lays in wait. When a spadefoot toad (which is about the same size as the larva) passes by, the larva grabs the toad's foot in its mouth. It then injects a poison into the toad's body before dragging its victim down into the mud. There it sucks all the body fluids from the toad and leaves the carcass to rot.

A Meal Of Tears

There is a small worm that lives under the eyelids of a hippopotamus. It feeds on the hippo's tears.

Bloodsuckers

The vampire moth of Malaysia sucks blood from animals. It has a long *proboscis* (mouthpart) which it drills into the skin of the animal. It then sucks up the blood and may remain doing this for up to an hour.

Female jigger fleas, which live in some of the southern parts of the USA, quite often burrow into the flesh of humans, usually beneath the toenails, where they feed on human blood until their eggs are ready for hatching.

Female bedbugs can suck up twice their own weight in blood and that can keep them living for as long as a year.

Yeeuch!

Houseflies feed by first spitting on the food. The juices break down the food into a pulp which the fly then soaks up for its meal.

Watch Out For Flying Cows

Germ warfare is not a new idea – it goes way back to the Middle Ages. In those days armies would catapult the carcasses of dead animals into the towns and castles they were attacking so that the rotting flesh would spread disease. Watch out! Here comes another cow!

CHAPTER FOUR

Foul Food

Table Manners

It was considered quite acceptable to belch at the table in medieval times – provided that you did not do so into someone's face. Nose picking was also permissible at the table but you had to take care to wipe the snot on your clothes and not on the tablecloth! Even spitting was allowed, provided that you spat on the floor and not on the table.

The Book Of Nature, a fifteenth-century work on etiquette by John Russell, gave servants this advice: "Do not claw your head or your back as if you were after a flea, or stroke your hair as if you sought a louse. Do not pick your nose or let it drop clear pearls. Do not pick your teeth. And do not lick a dish with tongue to get out dust."

In most modern societies it is considered extremely bad manners to belch after a meal, but in some countries it is regarded as an insult to the cook if you do not give out a good, loud belch.

Anne Boleyn, second queen of Henry VIII of England, had the habit of puking between courses at banquets. She employed a special maid to hold up a sheet as she vomited so it would not put off the other guests.

Peter the Great, Tsar of Russia from 1682 to 1725, had a rather disturbing habit at mealtimes. He would often walk on the table, treading on all the food and the cutlery.

Sick Of Drinking

A remedy advocated for addiction to alcohol in the nineteenth century was for the patient to drink a quart of warm water to which had been added a glass of spirits and something to make him sick. He would then be put into a large drum in a darkened room. The drum was to be revolved until the poor man puked violently. This cure was to be repeated every day until the patient decided to give up drinking.

An Unusual Breakfast

A leading Indian politician, Moraji Ranchodji Desai, began an unusual morning habit in 1971, when he decided to start each day by drinking a glass of his own urine. Some people thought he was potty and it was just a passing phase. It did not seem to do him any harm and he insisted that his morning beverage was a health-giving tonic.

In A Stew

A customer in a restaurant in Perth, Australia, complained that his stew had very little meat in it and demanded more. The waitress, Hannah Finlander, took the stew out into the kitchen, put a dead mouse in it, and returned it to the customer. Naturally she was dismissed from her job as a result.

Worms On The Menu

The Insect Club

There is a restaurant in America in which all the meals are made with worms, insects, and other strange gourmet delights. It is called the Insect Club and here you can dine on crickets in puff pastry, mealworms, spiders, ants, locusts, grubs, and many other items you would probably not want to know about. No more jokes about,

"Waiter, there's a fly in my soup" because in this restaurant it is meant to be there!

Down Mexico Way

Worms of all sorts are delicacies in many parts of the world. In Mexico they fry them and cover them with sugar. Also in Mexico, it is possible to buy worms from street sellers. The worms, which live on palm trees, have been fried in oil and then rolled in sugar.

Wriggly Quiche

Two thousand dishes of earthworms were set before judges in a contest in Pomana, California. The judges had to sample every one before they decided that the tastiest recipe of all was Earthworm Quiche Lorraine. Ordinary earth-worms are said to taste like Shredded Wheat.

Midnight Feasts

During his fourth voyage the crew on

Christopher Columbus's ship ate their meals at night so they could not see the worms wriggling around in the food.

Cackuccino

A very special and expensive coffee can be bought in Japan. It is made with beans that have passed through the digestive system of the palm civet wild cat, the droppings of which are sold in the markets of Sumatra.

Fancy A Locust?

Believe it or not, locusts are eaten in many parts of the world. They can be grilled, fried, covered in chocolate, made into cakes and, although they are a bit crunchy, they are reputed to be very nutritious.

Eating them could also prove beneficial to farmers, for, according to the British *entomologist* (insect expert) C.V. Riley, this is the best way of dealing with the swarms of locusts that destroy valuable crops.

To the Japanese and Chinese locusts are a delicacy. They are grilled or fried and then covered with a sauce and wrapped in pancakes.

Some people, however, object to eating locusts. They say that eating locusts isn't cricket.

Grubs As Grub

The people of New Guinea like nothing better than a dish of lightly roasted witchetty grubs.

Workers in Japanese silk factories are always assured of a handy snack for they cook and eat any grubs they find in the silkworm cocoons they look after.

The Truth About Cochineal

Cochineal, used as a food colouring, is made from the blood of scale insects from Mexico. Some 70,000 bodies are crushed and dried to a fine powder to make just fifty grams of dye. This makes it rather expensive so most modern cochineal is made chemically.

Snake Omelette

When Ursula Beckley of Long Island, USA, went to make an omelette in 1989 she received quite a shock. She was mixing three eggs together when she saw that one of them contained a six-inch-long black snake.

Devil's Dung For Dinner

The spice asafoetida, which is made from the sap of a plant that grows in parts of Asia, is popularly known as "devil's dung" because it is so stinky. Another name is "stinking gum". It smells sulphurous, like rotten eggs, but this changes into an onion-like smell when it is heated.

Asafoetida is added, in very small amounts, in cooking, especially to vegetarian meals and spicy dishes like curries. It adds to the taste of the dish, but one of the main reasons for its use is that it makes you less likely to fart after the meal. Perhaps it should be renamed asfartida powder?

And Horse Dung For Dinner

A popular salad dish in eighteenth-century Britain contained mustard and cress – and horse dung.

Drinks With Body

When the great British naval commander Horatio Nelson was killed at the Battle of Trafalgar in 1805 it was decided that he was such a national hero that he could not be buried at sea. To preserve the body until they got back to England it was placed in a barrel of brandy. But the brandy was not wasted. After Nelson's body was removed the crew drank it.

The Cocoma tribe of Peru used to grind up the bones of relatives and mix them into a strong drink.

When King Mausolus, ruler of Caria in Asia Minor, died in 353 BC his wife, Queen Artemisia, had his ashes mixed with wine, which she then drank.

Tickling Stick To Make You Sick

The Roman emperor Vitellus was renowned for

his gargantuan feasts. Between each course he used to stick a feather down his throat to make himself sick so he could eat even more.

King Of Gluttons

King Louis XIV, who was king of France for seventy-two years, was famous for the amount of food he ate. He ate so much it was said that he had a giant tapeworm in his gut.

Cena Molida

When you sit down in a restaurant it is always useful to know something about the food of the area. In a restaurant in Belize you could be tempted to try a local delicacy called Cena Molida. But before you do, just consider the fact that it contains mashed cockroaches!

Underpants To The Rescue

In 1994 the boat of a Filipono fisherman, Renato Arganza, capsized and he had to endure several days out at sea hanging on to a buoy. When he was rescued people were surprised that he had survived for so long. The fisherman explained that he had survived by eating his underpants. Let's hope he washed them first!

Elephant Stew

A Canadian wildlife magazine once gave its readers a recipe for elephant stew. It said. "Cut a medium-sized elephant into bite-size pieces, cover with brown gravy and cook for four weeks at 465 degrees. This serves 3,800 people but for more, add two rabbits."

The Man Of Many Tastes

The nineteenth-century geologist William Buckland boasted that he was prepared to eat anything that moved. To prove this claim he enjoyed meals of hedgehog, roast bear, and even puppy. He did admit that he was not over keen on roast mole.

Buckland's son Francis carried on this strange habit and formed the Society for the Acclimatization of Animals in the United Kingdom. Its aim was to educate the British

public on how food shortages could be avoided by eating different meats. He and his colleagues set the trend by dining on such delicacies as rhinoceros pie, slug soup, and boiled elephant trunk!

Adulterated Food

Down through the centuries there have been many occasions when unscrupulous traders put things into food to save themselves money or to make bigger profits. Many of the additions they used were extremely dangerous to the customer. Here are a few:

Milk sellers in the nineteenth century used to add chalk to the milk they sold to make it look whiter.

Publicans often added a substance called *cocculus indicus* to their beer to make it appear strong and flavoursome. Unfortunately the additive was also highly poisonous!

Butter that had gone off was given a thin coating of fresh butter to make it look good.

Pounded rice was added to sugar to make money.

Fishmongers in the Middle Ages put pigs' blood on stale fish to make it look fresh.

Fine brown earth was added to cocoa.

During the first half of the nineteenth century there was an ever-increasing demand for white bread, so many bakers added alum and other substances to their flour to make it whiter.

The War Loaf

In Britain during the First World War the government ordered that soya, potatoes, and cereals be added to flour to make it go further. This resulted in dark-coloured and rather nasty-tasting bread, which led to a declining bread consumption even after the war.

The chef Georges Auguste Escoffier described this bread as "more depressing than the plague of darkness and infinitely more dangerous than the air raids. One could hope to escape being hit by German bombs, but who could dodge the bulletproof crust and sour, soggy interior of a war loaf?"

Fish Of Death

Fugu, or puffer fish, is a great delicacy in Japan. But it is also highly poisonous and many people have died in agony within minutes of eating it. It has to be prepared by specially trained chefs who know how to take out the poison.

Anyone fancy a plate of fugu and chips?

How To Behave Like A Prince

There was a lot of fuss at a wedding reception in October 1999 when Prince Harry, son of His Royal Highness Prince Charles, apparently swallowed a goldfish.

Instead of the traditional flower arrangements the tables bore bowls of goldfish.

Guests were flabbergasted when the fifteen-year-old prince reached towards one of the bowls, took out a fish and swallowed it!

Although there was a lot of talk about whether or not he did really swallow a fish, and many thought the display was in very bad taste, they should have remembered the fact that Prince Harry has always been a lover of practical jokes.

You can try the same joke with just a piece of carrot. Cut a thin slice of carrot into the shape of a goldfish. It does not have to be very well made as people only see it for a second or two. Hide the carrot "fish" in your hand as you reach towards the goldfish bowl. Pretend to take a fish out of the bowl (do not actually put your hands in the water) but it is really the piece of carrot. Wiggle it a bit so it looks like a live fish and promptly eat it! Then wait for the reactions of amazement and disgust from everyone around you.

Core!

The eighteenth-century German poet and dramatist Friedrich von Schiller always kept a pile of rotten apples on his desk. Apparently they were there to give him inspiration for his writings, which included the hymn "Ode to Joy" and several plays. Often he just sniffed at the apples but sometimes he would eat one – surely more likely to give him stomach ache than inspiration!

Spit And Beansprouts, Please

Bird's nest soup is a favourite delicacy in China and other parts of the Far East. Believe it or not but it actually *is* made from a real bird's nest. The bird is the South-East Asian cave swiftlet, which makes its nest from saliva. The bird spits the saliva on to cave walls where it hardens. More spit is gradually added until the nest is formed. It is these nests of spit that are used to make bird's nest soup.

How to Grin And Bear It

Nimrod Robertson, a Yukon trapper, once shot a bear because there was nothing else available in the snowy wastes that was edible. There was just one big problem: Nimrod had lost all his

teeth! He solved the problem quite simply. He cut into the bear's mouth and extracted some of the creature's teeth, which he then fashioned into a primitive set of dentures so that he was able to eat the bear meat. That must be the only bear in history that was eaten by its own teeth!

Snake Juice

Food production is done under very strict hygiene conditions but occasionally something goes disgustingly wrong.

A man in Folkestone, England, once opened a bottle of stout and the head of a long snake came out. It was dead, perhaps dead drunk, but nobody could explain how it got there.

Fruit And Mouse Chocolate Bar

A man in Bedfordshire, England, bought a chocolate bar at an off-licence. He was enjoying it immensely when he started crunching on a nut. It seemed rather a large nut so he removed it from his mouth – it was the head of a mouse!

When the chocolate manufacturers were taken to court they said it was the first time anything like this had happened in over a hundred years.

The worrying thing, however, was that all

remaining stocks of that type of chocolate bar were removed from the shops and examined and there was no trace of the rest of the mouse. Presumably someone else had enjoyed their chocolate and mouse bar without realizing what they were eating!

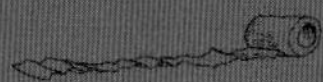

Beanes Means "Beings"

Sawney Beane and his large family lived in a cave near Galloway in fifteenth-century Scotland. They supported themselves by murdering and robbing any unwary traveller who happened to pass by. When they were eventually caught by King James I and 400 soldiers it was discovered that the Beanes had a gory secret. Inside their cave the soldiers found the remains of numerous human bodies hanging on the walls. Some of the body parts had even been pickled to preserve them. The Beanes were not only robbing and murdering their victims – they were eating them as well! The authorities decided not to have a trial, so the family were taken to Edinburgh where they were put to death in 1435.

Instead of eating human be-ins perhaps the Beanes should have stuck with baked beans?

Secret Of The Spicy Dumplings

The White Temple Restaurant in China was renowned for its spicy Szechuan dumplings. People flocked from far and wide to try them and many returned for more. The chef Wang Guang would not let anyone know his secret recipe. In 1991 the secret was revealed – the dumplings contained human flesh supplied by Guang's brother, who worked in the local crematorium. Perhaps he should have advertised his dumplings with the slogan "My dumplings have plenty of body in them."

Rats And Rice

In 1990 a most unusual restaurant was opened in Canton, China. It was called The Super Deer but deer was not on the menu, they only served rats. The owner, Zhang Guoxon, decided against calling it The Super Rat as he thought that might put customers off!

Steamed rat with rice, crispy fried rat, rat kebabs, and braised rat were among the many delicious dishes on offer.

Somewhat surprisingly the strange menu did not put people off and the restaurant became very popular. The customers may, however, have changed their minds if they had known how the rats were killed – they were boiled alive. Zhang Guoxon reckoned it was the most effective way to kill them.

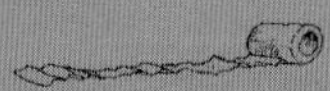

Cannibal Cookery

One of the most unusual cookery books in the world must be that written by the anthropologist Paul Shankman. It detailed the different ways that cannibals have cooked and eaten other humans.

A Real Family Butcher

Meat was very scarce and expensive in Berlin, Germany, during the 1920s. But Karl Denke always had a plentiful supply of smoked pork in his butcher's shop and it was quite cheap as well. Word soon got around and Denke did a roaring trade in his tasty meat.

The source of his cheap meat was discovered when police were called to stop a heated argument between Denke and one of his neighbours. During the course of their visit they happened to go into the back room of the shop. It turned out that his "smoked pork" was really human flesh and there were barrels of it in the back of the shop. Denke had killed at least fifty-two people to keep his shop supplied. Bet a few people in Berlin very quickly became vegetarians after they found out what they had been eating!

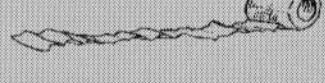

Meat From Two Legged "Horses"

There was another, similar, case in Hanover, Germany, at around the same time. A local meat dealer, Fritz Haarmann, did a roaring trade selling horse meat at the open market – until it was discovered that Haarmann's meat was not horse but human!

Sickening Sausages

Massive amounts of blood were donated in Britain during the Second World War to help heal injured people. In fact so much was given that the country had a surplus. At the same time there were serious food shortages, so scientists suggested that the surplus blood be made into black pudding, which could be given to the people to eat. The British Minister of Food, Lord Wooton, eventually decided that such a delicacy would not be appreciated by the general public!

Oysters Get Their Revenge

Vitellus, who was emperor of Rome in AD 69, was a greedy pig. He spent most of his day eating food of all sorts. He seemed to be particularly fond of oysters – it was said that he could eat as many as a thousand a day. The people of Rome rebelled against the emperor's selfishness (or should that be shell-fish-ness?) and he was deposed. They dumped his body in the River Tiber, where no doubt he became the food for the fishes that he himself had devoured so avidly during his lifetime.

Yum, Yum!

Another Roman glutton, by the name of Arpocras, once had a most unusual meal – four tablecloths and a broken glass!

Nasty Banquets

The feasts of the Roman emperor Heliogabalus, who lived in the second century AD, often included some unusual dishes. Apart from honeyed dormice he also served up camel feet and conger eels fattened in the flesh of Christian slaves. One meal consisted of the heads of 600 ostriches. But he did not expect his guests to eat the whole lot – they only ate the brains!

Horses For Courses

In 1855 a banquet for 132 people was held in Paris. Every course had horse meat in it. For starters there was vermicelli in horse meat broth. This was followed by sausages and roast horse meat and the main dishes were ragoût of horse meat, boiled horse meat, fillet of horse meat with mushrooms, and horse meat à la mode. The vegetables included potatoes fried in horse fat and a salad dressed with oil made from horse fat. And the pudding? Rum and horse marrow cake.

There weren't any speeches – the diners were too hoarse to speak.

Eggs-asperating Diets

Piero di Cosimo, a fifteenth-century painter, ate nothing but boiled eggs. He must have been quite constipated with all that cholesterol bunging up his tubes. And with all that sulphur in his system he probably suffered with flatulence as well!

The Victorian artist Richard Dadd enjoyed a similar diet. For several years he lived on hard-boiled eggs and beer. At least the beer would have helped him go to the toilet!

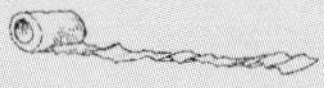

CHAPTER FIVE

Vile Bodies

Stiff Upper Lip

When Queen Elizabeth I of England lost her front teeth she stuffed her mouth with cloth so it would not look sunken.

Mucky Monks

During the Middle Ages the Cistercian monks were forbidden to bath – except at Christmas and Easter.

Beauty From The Botty

Camel dung rubbed in your hair will make the hair wavy – so it is said. If you try it and it doesn't work please don't get the hump.

Hen poo was once used to cure skin problems.

In Britain soap made from pig manure

was quite commonly used until the late 1930s. It had a strong smell but people got used to it.

According to Elizabethan belief puppy wee helps to improve the complexion. But you do not put it on your skin – you drink it!

Saintly Fleas

When the body of St Thomas à Becket, Archbishop of Canterbury, was prepared for burial in 1170 his robes were found to "seethe" with fleas.

You've Been Collared

Medieval lords and ladies wore neckpieces of fur or feathers to trap fleas. When the collar became full of the little creatures it was given to a servant to empty.

A Short Poem About Fleas

Adam
'ad 'em.

A Horrendous Hairpiece

The seventeenth-century diarist Samuel Pepys found nits in his wig. In those days that was not a surprising occurrence, except for the fact that the wig was a new one he had just bought.

Ode To A Louse

The Scottish poet Robert Burns wrote his *Ode To A Louse* after sitting behind a lady in church who had a superb hairstyle – except for the fact that it was infested with lice. It contains the famous lines:

"O wad some Pow'r the giftie gie us

To see oursels as others see us!
It wad frae mony a blunder free us."

Suffering For Beauty

Ringing Necks

In some parts of Burma it was the fashion for the Padaung or Karen women to have extremely long necks covered with copper rings. The rings would be added one at a time over a period until the neck was as long as 40 cm (15 inches).

Saucer Lips

It was the fashion in some parts of Africa for women to put large wooden saucers into their lower lips. The practice started as a way to make the women unattractive to slave traders but eventually became regarded as a sign of beauty!

Long Lobes

Long ear lobes were the fashion in some parts of Africa. Rings were inserted into the ear lobes of young girls and over a period of years larger and larger rings would be put in until the lobes were several inches long.

Bathing In Milk

Queen Cleopatra of Egypt is said to have bathed in ass's milk to give her a nice complexion. No doubt the milk was thrown away afterwards, but the Duke of Queensbury, who lived from 1724 to 1810, was not so wasteful. He bathed in milk every day but the milk was then sold to the general public. Perhaps they liked their milk with plenty of body in it?

Some Day My Prints Will Come

The American bank robber John Dillinger hit upon a marvellous scheme to outwit the police.

He knew his fingerprints were on file so he dipped his fingers in acid to erase the telltale lines on his fingertips. It caused him excruciating pain but he felt it was worth it. Unfortunately it didn't work – when the skin healed, his fingerprints were exactly the same as they were before. His career, and his life, ended in 1934 when he was shot and killed by the FBI in Chicago.

The Great Unwashed

Beethoven

The great German composer Ludwig van Beethoven was too engrossed in producing musical masterpieces to worry about how dirty his clothes became. This got so bad that friends had to take away his filthy clothes to be washed while he was asleep.

Chairman Mao

The Chinese leader Mao Tse-Tung stopped brushing his teeth, saying that tigers never brushed theirs. And he never washed either, so it must have been quite a smelly experience to meet him in later life.

Frederick The Great

King Frederick II, Frederick the Great, of Prussia did not like water so it was not very often that he had a wash. Even though he was king of Prussia he must have whiffed a bit. Frederick never bothered to change his clothes in old age. Upon his death a servant had to put his own shirt on the king because the king's had rotted with sweat. There was also a cleaning-up job to do after the king's death because much of the palace floor was covered with the excrement of the king's pack of greyhounds.

Charles II

In the seventeenth century many people believed that washing your face caused toothache and baldness. This worried King Charles II of England so much that he only dabbed his cheeks with water before getting dressed each day.

Louis XIII

Another stinky king must have been Louis XIII of France. It is said that he had only five baths in the whole of his life. Phew!

The 11th Duke of Norfolk

When the 11th Duke of Norfolk became incredibly smelly because he never bathed his servants would get him drunk and give him a quick wash before he knew what was going on.

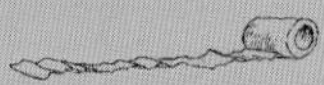

Soliman's Water

In the sixteenth century many people used a lotion called Soliman's Water to treat their skin and to get rid of spots, warts and even freckles. It probably did the job because it contained mercury which burned off the skin. It also had the undesirable side effect of making one's teeth fall out!

Surreal Scent

A perfume made of fish glue and cow dung was worn by the Spanish painter Salvador Dali to impress his girlfriend Gala. He must have ponged a bit.

It's In His Kiss

Whenever humans kiss they exchange some 40,000 germs. Yuck!

What A Grind

It used to be the custom in the East Indies to file one's teeth down to the gums as part of a wedding ceremony and during mourning.

Waterloo Choppers

It was the fashion in Regency England to have dentures made from "Waterloo teeth". These were teeth pulled from the corpses on the battlefield.

Smelly Feet Facts

In parts of northern England in the nineteenth century women were warned not to wash their feet while they were expecting a baby. It was thought that washing one's feet could harm the unborn child. The smell of the unwashed feet probably did it even more harm!

Smelly feet attract mosquitoes according to research carried out at Wageningen Agricultural University in Holland. Researcher Bart Knols sat beneath a mosquito net wearing just his underpants. When the mosquitoes were released three-quarters of them made for his feet. So, if you don't want to be bitten by mosquitoes, better wash your feet.

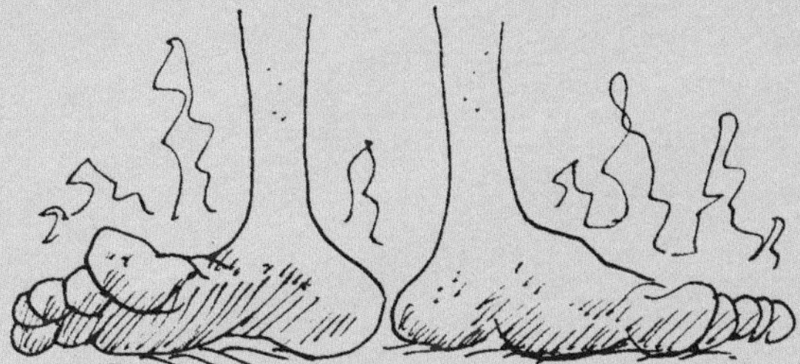

Crumbs!

Poppea, the wife of the Roman emperor Nero, put on a face mask made from breadcrumbs and ass's milk at night. Perhaps she wanted to be the toast of the town.

Would You Use This Face Pack?

A recipe for a face pack in Georgian times contained liquid from a cucumber, white flowers, lemon juice, and seven or eight pigeons which had been plucked, beheaded, and finely minced. It was said to improve the complexion – if anyone had the nerve to try it.

Howdy, Pale Face

When he was Prince Regent, George IV, who was king of Britain from 1820 to 1830, often had blood drawn from his body. He did so to make himself look pale and elegant.

The Face Of Death

It was fashionable in the eighteenth century for ladies to have a white complexion. Lady Maria Coventry was one of the women who went along with this fashion and obtained a lovely white skin. To achieve this she put a special powder on her face but, alas, it was to contribute to her death. The main ingredient of the powder was white lead. This is deadly poisonous and caused Lady Maria to die of lead poisoning.

Swallow That!

In 1960 surgeons in America found 258 different items in a patient's stomach. These included 88 coins, 39 nail files, 3 pairs of tweezers, 3 metal chains, a bracelet, a 3 lb piece of metal, 26 keys, religious medals, 4 nail clippers, a necklace, and 3 sets of rosary beads!

Mouse Brows

The fashionable men and women of the English court in the eighteenth century used to shave

off their eyebrows. They then replaced them with false eyebrows made of mouse skin. Fish glue was used to fix them to the brows.

Germs Everywhere

You pick up some 300,000,000 germs on your hands every day. It must get pretty crowded on your skin at times.

Poisoned Pupils

Italian women used to use *deadly nightshade* as eye drops to make their pupils dilate to look more attractive. The plant is also known as *belladonna* (beautiful lady) because of this (another explanation of the name is that it came about because an Italian poisoner named Leucota used it to kill beautiful women). Either way the plant is one to be avoided – as its name suggests, it is highly poisonous.

Mummy's Boy

King Charles II collected powder from Egyptian mummies and rubbed it on himself. He believed

it would give him "ancient greatness" but it probably just made him rather dusty and stinky.

Ants In Their Eyes

The ancient Egyptians used an eye make-up made from crushed ants' eggs.

CHAPTER SIX

Biology Bits

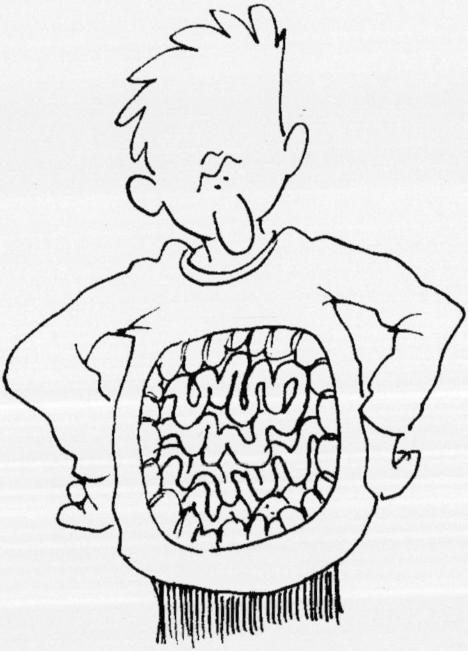

What's A Wart?

A wart is a lump of fibres covered with skin, usually on the hands. It is caused by a virus which enters the skin and causes the skin cells to multiply quickly.

Warts can be spread by touch or by contact with another piece of skin from a wart. They are usually painless, but can be unsightly. It is possible to remove warts on the hands by the use of special paint obtainable from a chemist's shop.

A wart on the underside of the foot is known as a verruca and these can be painful. Verruca is actually the Latin word for "wart" – just thought you'd like to know that.

If the paint does not work, or if the wart is on any part of the body other than the hands or feet, consult a doctor.

Another Remedy

Robert Zabercky, a twelve-year-old boy from Burbank, California, had forty-seven warts on his hands. His father paid out hundreds of dollars on medical bills in an effort to get rid of them but nothing worked. A fortnight after Robert visited relatives in Ayrshire, Scotland, the warts had disappeared. The boy had discovered a most unusual remedy. Every day for two weeks he went into the local fields and rubbed his skin with cow dung – it worked!

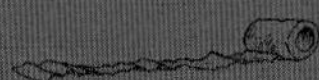

Bugged Beds

Good night,
Sleep tight,
Don't let the bedbugs bite

Lots of mums send their kids to bed saying that. But did you know that there really are such

things as bedbugs? They are flat, wingless bugs up to 6 mm (1/4 inch) in length that live in your bed. During the night they gorge themselves on your blood and they keep hidden during the day. They are flat, which means that they can hide in the tiniest cracks and crevices.

So if you hear any chomping noises during the night it might be the bedbugs having a midnight feast – and the main dish on the menu is you!

Do You Think You Are Clean?

You probably think you are very clean when you have had a wash. Don't you believe it. No matter how hard you scrub there are still millions of bacteria on your body – some two million on your face alone.

What About The Rest?

We carry about 55 grams (2 ounces) of dirt on our bodies but having a bath only rids us of half of this. So what happens to the rest?

Bathing Is Dangerous

Too many baths can remove natural protective oils and salts produced by your skin glands, which can lower your resistance to disease and cause skin dryness – a good excuse if your mother tells you to have a bath and you can't be bothered.

You Are Not Alone

Feeling Lousy

Head lice live in the hair and suck blood from your skin. They are often spread among schoolchildren and the school authorities have to be told if a child has them. Although they are tiny, they are visible, and it is not unknown to see them jumping around. The eggs of the head lice are called nits. These look like tiny white spots hanging on the hair. There are several ways of getting rid of head lice and nits, including special lotions – probably the safest way is to soak your hair in conditioner every few days and then comb it through with a very fine comb, often called a nit comb.

No Fun With Fungi

Fungi, microscopic growths invisible to the naked eye, like to live in warm, humid areas of the body. So they are more likely to be between the toes, in the groin, under the arms, or on the head. They live by feeding on organic matter such as dead skin. They cause no harm until they have such favourable conditions that they develop and multiply rapidly. Often they get on to the body because people do not take enough care. Walking barefoot on the beach or in public showers are good ways to pick up fungi. Wearing clothes used by others is also a way to get infected. Cutting down on the perspiration in the feet and groin areas by wearing appropriate clothing reduces the risk. And if you itch don't scratch it (easier said than done), as this can spread the fungi from place to place. The principal way to stop fungi getting out of hand (you will never get rid of them completely) is exactly the same as the cure – keep the skin as clean and dry as you can. If problems continue, go to see a doctor, who may have to experiment with different kinds of medication until the right one is found.

Itchy Skin

Scabies is a skin disorder that causes intense itching. When you scratch the itch to try and get some relief you eventually damage the skin, which causes sores and scabs to form. The disease is caused by the scabies, or itch, mite,

which burrows into the skin. It then lays eggs under the skin and more mites are hatched. To get rid of them all affected areas have to be scrubbed with an insecticide prescribed by a doctor.

Flea For All

Fleas usually live on a specific animal. Animal fleas will not stay long on human skin but they can bite and suck your blood, which makes the skin very itchy for a couple of days. Fleas usually hatch in bedding about a week after their eggs have been laid. They will then continue to live in your bed, feeding off your pet and you! Anti-flea sprays on the pet and on the bedding should get rid of most of them. You may also have to put a flea repellent on your skin so you do not get bitten.

Human fleas love warm blood, especially yours! To get this they drill a sharp, needle-like siphon through your skin and then start sucking, just like sucking orange juice up through a straw.

A flea can jump as far as 33 cm (13 inches) and to a height of 20 cm (8 inches) – that's equivalent to a man jumping a length of almost 150 metres (500 feet) and to a height of 90 metres (300 feet)!

Mine Host

Although small the flea has other even smaller parasites living on and in it. The famous eighteenth-century writer Jonathan Swift wrote about this:

So, naturalists observe, a flea
Hath smaller fleas that on him prey;
And these have smaller fleas to bite 'em.
And so proceed ad infinitum.

No Need To Pick Your Nose

Your nose has lots of *mucus* in it. Mucus is a sticky substance in which scent particles dissolve so you can smell. It also traps the muck you breathe in so it doesn't go down your tubes to bung up your lungs.

But all this mucus has to go somewhere. When you blow your nose or sneeze you get rid of some of it, and about a quarter of it is swallowed (how disgusting!).

So there is no longer any need to pick your nose and eat it (a disgusting habit at the best of times) because your body is doing it for you automatically.

The reason it does this is that the nose produces about 2½ litres (4 pints) of moisture a day. If this remained in the nasal passages it would stagnate so, every twenty or so minutes, a new film of mucus is produced and the old film is swallowed, complete with any bacteria it contains.

Everyone's A Nose Picker

Picking your nose is considered to be a rather disgusting habit. This is rather strange because everyone does it!

How To Be Utterly Disgusting

Get a piece of soft (chewed) chewing gum in your left hand. Start picking your nose with your right fingers then bring up the left hand to cover your nose (be careful not to put any gum inside your nose).

The right fingers now pull down the chewing

gum so it looks like snot coming from your nose. Now pop it in your mouth and chew it. Ugh! Don't be surprised if your mother tells you off for doing this!

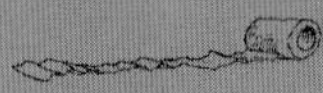

Nice And Sneezy

Cold Feet Can Make You Sneeze

The heat mechanism of the nose is similar to that of the feet. When your feet are cold so are the nasal membranes. When cold, the membranes produce more mucus and you sneeze to clear the nasal passages. Perhaps that is why an old cure for a cold was to soak the feet in hot water.

Eyes Wide Open

Did you know that it is impossible to sneeze with your eyes open? It's just as well because they would probably rupture and fall out!

Don't Sneeze, Please

When you sneeze thousands of tiny droplets are shot out of your nose at speeds of up to 165 km (100 miles) per hour. If you drove at that speed you'd get done for speeding!

Get anyone standing nearby to carry an umbrella or they are likely to get a little wet!

Handkerchief Catch

The mucus you sneeze out contains bacteria and can spread some infections. A British government information film in the 1950s tried to draw attention to this spreading of infection with the slogan, "Coughs and sneezes spread diseases. Catch them in your handkerchief."

Ear Today, Gone Tomorrow

In 1971 Benedikt Auren, a Viennese farmer, joked to a friend, "I bet you daren't bite off my ear." The friend accepted the bet and ended up being charged with assault.

Down In The Mouth

Most people have a problem with bad breath at one time or another. Sometimes it is caused by

food we have eaten but often it is a sign that something is wrong.

Bad breath is quite common in the early morning because your saliva glands slow down their production while you are asleep, so you are not getting your normal mouthwash. Once you are awake the glands go back to normal production.

Everyone knows that garlic remains on the breath for a long time after it is eaten, as do spicy foods like curries, but other foods can cause bad breath as well. Garlic will stay on your breath for almost a day and curry for perhaps eighteen hours. Onions are a little better as their smell lasts only about half a day. Dairy products such as cheese, milk, ice cream, and things made with them, can remain on your breath for half an hour or more. The same is true of eggs and oily fish, such as mackerel or herring.

But what if you haven't been eating garlic, or curry, or whatever? Well, bad breath can also be caused by bad teeth so it pays to look after them. Gum disease is another cause, as is catarrh at the back of the nose. Consistently bad-smelling breath could also be an indication of diabetes or even kidney disease.

The best way to keep your breath smelling fresh is regular brushing of the teeth, followed by a good rinsing of the mouth. If the bad breath persists (and your friends will be sure to tell you), a visit to the dentist may be needed. If that fails and the bad breath still continues, go to your doctor.

It's A Cracker

Cracking one's knuckles is said to be in bad taste but a man named Slats Grobnik became quite famous for it. He started cracking his knuckles as a teenager and found he could do it louder than anyone else. His mother took him to a doctor in Chicago, who simply said that the boy had loud knuckles. So loud were the cracks he produced that he was sometimes employed as a starter at athletics meetings because his knuckles were better than a starting pistol!

Apparently the cracking is nothing to do with the bones but is caused by tiny gas bubbles that form in the joints. When the fingers are bent forward the gas makes a popping sound, often to the annoyance of anyone within earshot.

A Swallow Proved Your Innocence

No doubt you have noticed that when you are nervous or afraid the saliva (spit to you) in your mouth seems to dry up.

Judges in the Middle Ages sometimes used this fact as a sort of lie detector test, to determine whether a suspect was guilty or innocent. Flour was put into the suspect's mouth. If he was innocent he would produce enough saliva to enable him to swallow the flour. But if he was guilty his mouth would dry up with fright and he would not be able to swallow.

Dining On Bacteria

Every time you swallow, you swallow millions and millions of bacteria. This sounds horrible but it is part of the body's cleaning process. Your saliva glands produce saliva, which attacks and kills the bacteria in your mouth. These are then disposed of by swallowing.

Night-Time Noise

A good snore can hit a level of sixty-nine decibels – that's almost as loud as a pneumatic drill.

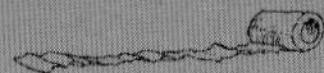

How To Protect Yourself

Ever wondered why you are sick or get diarrhoea? It is your body's way of protecting you if you have eaten any contaminated food or have over-indulged.

Your body is always trying to protect you from illness. If you get a splinter in your finger, for example, a protective blister often forms over the wound. This can be quite painful but eventually the blister bursts and the splinter is thrown out of the skin.

If you get a fever you often sweat. This again is your body protecting you. Blood rushes to the surface of the skin to cool off and the sweat cools the skin.

If you are cold your body starts to shiver to warm itself up.

And if you are not feeling too good, your body forces you to rest as this is the best way to get better.

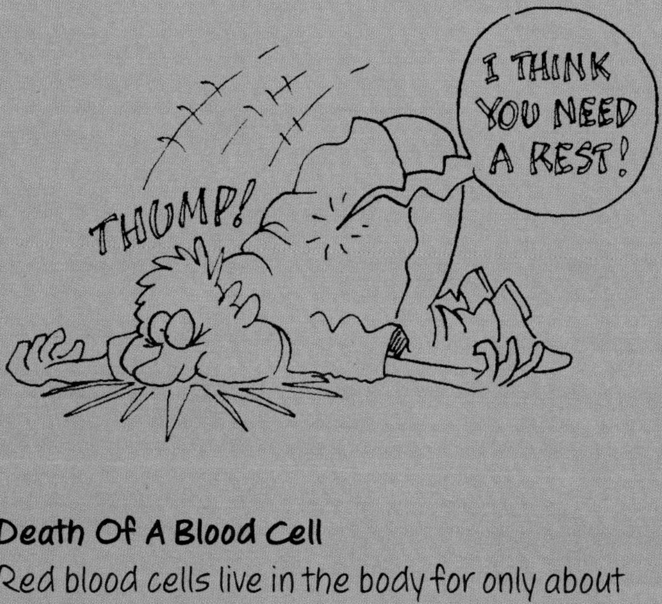

Death Of A Blood Cell

Red blood cells live in the body for only about four months. They are being devoured at the rate of nine million a second. Luckily the body is also producing new ones at the same rate.

About a ton of red blood cells will be produced by your body in your lifetime.

Blood cells end their life in the liver or the spleen. Here special cells called *phagocytes* (which means "cell eaters") engulf the blood cells and break them up. However, much of the cell material is recycled.

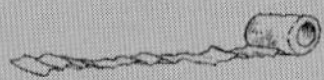

Anti-Germ Warfare

There is a continuous fight against germs taking place in your bloodstream. If germs or bacteria enter the body the white blood cells (or *leucocytes*) in your blood go on the attack. They flow over the germs and literally swallow them by folding themselves around the invaders. Once the bacteria have been completely absorbed the leucocytes go off in search of more germs to attack.

It's Good To Be Scabby

When you cut yourself your blood rushes to the spot to heal the wound and fight infection. Some of the blood clots on the surface of the skin and eventually forms a scab. It is very tempting, but you should never pick that scab off. It is protection for the new skin being formed underneath.

Food Fact

The stomach of an adult person can hold about 1.5 litres (2.5 pints) of food.

Getting Facts Back To Front

Which do you think is bigger – your large intestine or your small intestine?

In fact your large intestine is smaller than your small intestine. Believe it or not, it is true: the small intestine is about seven metres in length whereas the large intestine is only about two metres long!

Shedding Skin

Every minute of the day you are shedding skin cells. Some 40,000 dead skin cells come off your body every day. As much of the dust in the air consists of dead skin, you are continually breathing in bits of yourself (and other people). This dead skin also falls into your bed, on the floor, and on chairs on which you sit, providing a great meal for the millions of dust mites that live with you.

During your life you will drop some 18 kg (40 pounds) of dead skin. That's about the same weight as a five-year-old child.

Mal De Mer

Many people suffer from seasickness. Even the great Admiral Nelson often threw up when at sea. We tend to blame this outpouring of puke on our stomach but it is really our ears that cause it. Inside the ear there are three *semicircular canals,* which give us our sense of balance. These canals contain a liquid called *endolymph,* which sloshes around as we move. Nerve endings in the ears are stimulated by all this sloshing and send messages to the brain that something is going wrong. This results in dizziness and often causes people to puke.

Rumble Tum

Ever had a rumbling tummy? It is caused by gas in the intestines and the technical term for it is *borborygmus.*

Stone Me!

Stones can form in the gall bladder, the bag in your guts which collects bile. Bile is a yucky, greenish-brown liquid produced by the liver and stored in the gall bladder. A gallstone starts as a small piece of solid matter which grows as more material is gathered on it. Most gallstones are small but very sharp, like little crystals. Sometimes they can grow quite large and smooth.

Most gallstones do not have any effect on the person, they just stay quite happily in the gall bladder. Sometimes, however, they can travel along with the bile and get stuck in the bile duct, which can prove very painful and may make the person vomit.

Acid Drops

Did you know that you've got hydrochloric acid in your stomach? You produce two litres of the stuff every day and it is so powerful that it could dissolve metal.

As this acid is so strong you may wonder why the stomach doesn't dissolve itself. On the other hand, you may not wonder about this at all because, being something of a genius, you already know that the stomach wall is lined with a sticky mucus which protects it.

Sometimes, however, the gastric juices do break through this protective barrier when it has been injured in some way and the result is an ulcer. It is even possible for much of the stomach lining to be destroyed in this way, but the pain from ulcers can be so great that the patient will invariably have consulted a doctor before this stage is reached.

Enough To Make You Spit

Next time you go into a supermarket look at the bottles of milk and see how much 3 pints (1.71 litres) is. That is how much spit the average

human being produces in a day. In the course of a lifetime that adds up to an amazing 8,000 gallons (36,400 litres). Just think of that the next time your mouth is feeling dry.

Now imagine just 200 litre bottles of milk on your doorstep. That's the amount of sweat produced by the feet of the average adult male in a year.

CHAPTER SEVEN

Doing What Comes Naturally

Poo Production

During your life you will eat around fifty tonnes of food. Most of that is used to fuel your body for only about three tonnes comes out of the other end as poo.

Also during your life you are likely to drink around 42,000 litres of liquid. You do not retain

as much of that as you do food for some 27,000 litres will pass out as urine.

Proportionate Plop

Faeces (that's poo to you) are almost 90 per cent water.

Weights And Measures

The average stool (piece of poo) of an adult human weighs about 113 grams (4 ounces). An interesting snippet of information to throw into your next serious conversation with someone.

Roughly half of the poo you produce is made of the dead bodies of the bacteria from inside your gut. The rest is the material that could not be absorbed by the intestines and the lubricating mucus they produce.

The average person wees over 5,000 litres (2,800 gallons) of urine during his or her lifetime.

Useful Urine

In days gone by, housewives put urine to a variety of uses. Woollen clothes, blankets, and stockings would be trampled in a tub of fermented urine to get rid of the dirt and grease before rinsing (thoroughly, hopefully!). Bed linen was treated in the same way although people often complained about the smell when they got into bed.

Urine was also used for cleaning iron stoves and for scrubbing stone floors. When mixed with bracken ash it made a good polish for pewter.

Right up until the twentieth century many people in Britian washed their face and body in urine. Urine was free whereas soap was expensive, and wee was also more gentle than the soap of the day.

Throughout the centuries and in many different countries wee was used to wash the hair. Roman hairdressers used stale urine, known as "lotium", to wash people's hair. This practice continued until well into the seventeenth century.

Dipping the hands and feet in pee was once regarded as a protection from witchcraft. The Irish sprinkled children with it to keep them safe from fairies.

Washing children in their own widdle and giving them some of it to drink was once a common way of reducing fever in Europe and America.

The French believed that if a patient's urine was used in the making of a loaf of bread, the person who ate the bread would "take" the fever from the patient. A similar remedy was to boil an egg in the patient's wee. When the egg was eaten by another person the fever would be taken away.

Schoolboys used to use their wee as invisible ink!

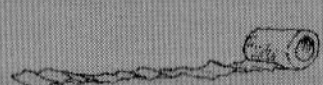

Water Pistol

It was the practice in eighteenth-century England to pee down the barrel of one's shotgun. This removed any rust around the tinder hole.

Money For Pee

In Roman times pee was collected in pots on street corners and sold to cloth manufacturers. They used it for stiffening and dyeing cloth.

Learn In The Lavatory

In 1975 a Japanese manufacturer produced toilet rolls with English lessons printed on them. It was said that regular users of the paper could learn 800 English words in the first year of using the paper. A spokesman for the company

said that "sitting where they are will give them time to use their brains profitably".

In the same year, a German toilet paper manufacturer marketed the same idea with twenty-six English lessons on each roll. To prevent family arguments the course was repeated eight times on every roll.

Who Flung Dung?

In September 1992 the housing offices of a local council in England were plastered with liquid farm manure. There was so much of the smelly liquid that the building ended up surrounded by a three-metre lake of dung.

The slurry had been sprayed on the building by a local farmer, Dave Cannon, as a complaint about the council's fourth rejection of his plans to build a retirement home on his land.

The protest caused quite a stink, in more ways than one, but unfortunately the manure had been aimed at the wrong building. The planning office, the real source of his dispute, was on the other side of the road!

In Canada a man staged a similar protest

when he was not allowed to renew his pilot's licence. He flew over the city of Calgary and "bombed" it with piles of pig poo.

The Great Stink

In the summer of 1858 the smell of raw sewage on the streets of London and the banks of the River Thames became so bad that it was discussed in parliament. Because the Houses of Parliament are on the banks of the Thames, the curtains had to be soaked in chloride of lime to allow the politicians to breathe.

Watch Out For The Pee!

Before toilets became commonplace in the home it was the usual practice to empty chamber pots out of the window and into the street below. It could get pretty wet and sticky if you were not carrying an umbrella! In France it was the custom to give a warning before chucking the urine out. They would shout "Gardez l'eau!" which, roughly translated, means "Watch out for the pee!".

In medieval cities the waste from toilets ran into open sewers that flowed through the streets and into the local river. Although the streets must have been really smelly, the people were generally happy with the system. What the people living downstream, where all the effluent finally came to rest, thought about it was a different matter.

What A Pong!

A book published around 1500 suggested that women should use cow dung as a deodorant!

A Long Drop For Plop

Toilets in the sixteenth century often consisted of just a small cupboard built into the wall. Sometimes the toilet was built into a special buttress on the outside of the main wall. There was a hole upon which the person sat and anything he or she produced simply went through the hole straight to the ground, or in some cases a moat, below. As a result the moat of a castle was often quite a smelly and insanitary place.

A good example of this can be seen at Acton

Court, a house built around 1534, near Bristol, England. Another one can be seen at Castle Stalker, near Fort William in Scotland, where the waste products had a thirty-metre drop straight into the sea.

All At Sea

Navy ships in the nineteenth century had toilets that were rather similar in principle to those of the medieval castles. They were simply a plank, or planks, with holes in them in front of the bow of the ship. All the waste material simply dropped through the holes and straight into the sea.

Sometimes the toilets, or "heads" as they were called because they were in the head of the ship, were quite close to the waterline and in rough weather sea water rushed up through the holes. Probably a good way to get your bum washed!

No Bathing

Queen Victoria was being shown around Cambridge University when she spotted lots of bits of paper floating in the River Cam. What she did not know was that the town sewers emptied straight into the river and what she was looking at were bits of toilet paper.

She asked her guide, Dr Whewell, what the papers were. Without blinking an eye he calmly replied, "Those, ma'am, are notices that bathing is forbidden."

In An English Country Garden

The song *An English Country Garden* was very popular in Britain – so popular that it was not long before someone put some rather rude words to the chorus:

What do you do, if you want to do a poo
In an English country garden?
Take down your pants, and suffocate the ants
In an English country garden.

There are several other verses along similar lines. One is:

What do you do, if you want to do a poo
In an English country garden?
Do it on a log and blame it on the dog
In an English country garden.

The final chorus is:

What do you do when you've done a little poo
In an English country garden?
Pick up a leaf and wipe your underneath
In an English country garden.

Going To Pot

Chamber pots, or potties, or gozunders (because it goes-under the bed) have been with us for thousands of years. They can prove very handy in the middle of the night when you have to go to the toilet but do not fancy a walk to the loo (especially in the days when toilets were often outside in the cold).

Potty Portraits

Potties in the early nineteenth century often had portraits of people in their bases. The idea was that you did your business over someone you disliked. Sounds like a good idea!

Potted Manure

Farmers in the nineteenth century went from house to house collecting the contents of the chamber pots. It made good fertilizer for their fields!

A World Of Constipation

People suffer more with *constipation* (difficulty in doing a poo) in the rich countries of the world than they do in poor countries. This is partly to do with diet but the main reason is that rich people sit on toilets and poor people tend just to squat wherever they are. Sitting while trying to have a poo is a bad position because the body leaning forward causes a sharp angle between the *rectum* (end of the large intestine) and the *anus* (through which the poo has to travel). To get it round this angle the sitter has to push, which results in leaning forward even more and makes the job harder still.

When squatting, however, there is an almost straight journey for the poo to travel. The muscles do not have to strain so hard and even gravity lends a hand (if you will excuse the expression).

Constipation And Diarrhoea

All people are different when it comes to emptying their bowels. Most people go once a day but others go only once a week. The more often one goes the more liquid are the faeces (another interesting fact to put into your conversation at the dinner table).

If the poo is almost completely liquid and the person is having to go a great deal more frequently than usual, and perhaps is experiencing stomach pains, then they probably have *diarrhoea*.

At the other end of the spectrum is *constipation*, which involves a difficulty in going to the toilet and stools that are hard and difficult to get out.

Constipation and diarrhoea are not in themselves illnesses but they could be an indication that something else is wrong (usually diet, but stress and other factors also play a part). A change of diet when you go on holiday, eating too many prunes, taking medicines, eating too much or too little fibre, or even the worry of school exams can all make a difference. Neither need cause the person any worry unless they persist for a while (diarrhoea for more than two days or constipation for a fortnight). Then it may be necessary to see a doctor.

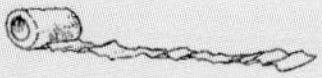

All Fall In

During a banquet given by Emperor Ferdinand in Erfurt, Germany, in 1184, the floor collapsed and many members of royalty, knights and nobles were dropped into the cesspit below. Some 806 years later, in September 1990, the joint wedding of two Jordanian brothers came to a similar messy end when the dance floor collapsed during the reception.

Live Loo

In 1995 a man was electrocuted in Ryde, on the Isle of Wight, as he sat on a loo. Unbeknown to him the metal lavatory seat on which he sat was live because of a faulty cable.

Other Words For The Lav

In Britain various words are used for the lavatory. These include "loo", "the smallest room", "bog", "WC" (water closet), "khazi" and "toilet".

In Australia the most used word is "dunny" and Americans often refer to it as "the John" or "the can".

A Poo By Any Other Name Would Smell As Sweet

There are lots of words for faeces in English. These include "excreta", "ordure", "poo", "plop", and "number twos". What do you call yours?

Pee Soup

Some of the words used for urine in English include "pee", "Jimmy Riddle", "piddle", "slash", "wee" and "number ones", among others.

What A Load Of Bumph

Most people who use the word "bumf" (or "bumph") to describe a lot of paper have no idea as to how this word came about. In fact it was originally used just for toilet paper, for the word is an abbreviation of "bum fodder". It probably originated in the mid-nineteenth century among schoolboys and soldiers.

At Wellington College, England, they have a paper chase which is known as the *bumf-hunt*.

These days you have to be careful what you say – you could be saying something rude without even knowing it!

Ancestral Piles

German farmers used to put piles of poo from their animals and from humans in front of their houses. The size of the pile showed the neighbour how rich the farmer was – the bigger the pile the more affluent the family (or perhaps that should be "the more effluent the family").

Astral Wee

The first American astronaut was Alan Sheppard and his initial flight on 5 May 1961 proved to be rather uncomfortable. The flight in the Mercury capsule was to take only fifteen minutes but unfortunately there were several technical problems which delayed blast-off for over four hours. During all of this time Sheppard remained in the capsule, clothed in a bulky spacesuit which restricted his movements.

Since the flight was expected to be short, there had been no need to think about toilet arrangements. But after four hours Sheppard announced that his bladder was bursting – he badly needed to have a pee. He warned mission control of the dilemma – he could not get out of the capsule because that would delay the mission even further and there was no way he could get out of his spacesuit to relieve himself.

The only answer was that he had to do it in his suit but mission control were worried

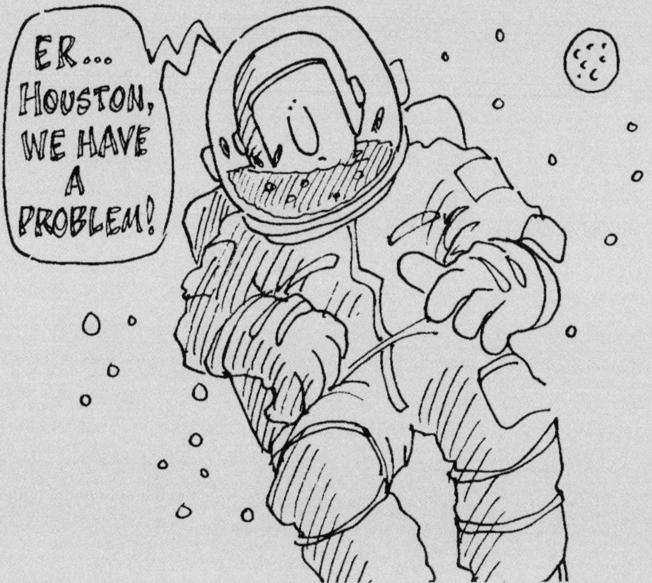

because there were many electrical contacts in the suit to monitor various aspects of the trip and the astronaut's reaction to them. It was feared that the urine would cause an electrical short and that this in turn could cause a fire in the capsule. After a long, agonizing delay they gave Sheppard permission to wee in his suit.

The urine did cause some of the sensors to

cut out but apart from that there was no damage. However, it proved uncomfortable for the astronaut as the urine ran inside the suit all over his stomach and ended up in a clammy pool in the small of his back. Eventually permission came for blast-off and the mission proved successful – if a little wet!

Crappy Nappy

In the early days of space flight the problem of adequate toilet facilities had not been solved so the astronauts had to wear nappies. Later they had more elaborate devices but there was often the problem that clouds of urine formed and floated around the spacecraft. The various problems have gradually been solved but even as late as the 1970s and 1980s, with the Skylab missions, there were still a few glitches. Sometimes bits of excreta would float around in the cabin. As the astronauts also playfully flicked bits of food around, everyone had to be careful in taking a floating morsel to eat. You could not tell what it was until you tasted it!

Modern astronauts do not have this problem as wee and poo is collected in bags (a bit like the ones you find in vacuum cleaners).

Lunar Pee

The American astronaut Buzz Aldrin claimed to be the first man to pee his pants on the moon.

Yuri's Urine

Russian cosmonauts pee on one of the tyres of the bus that takes them to the launch pad before they blast off into space. It is said that this tradition stems from the fact that the first cosmonaut, Yuri Gagarin, had to relieve himself before he made his epic orbit of the earth in *Vostok* in April 1961.

One Good Turd Deserves Another

Moulay Ismael, sultan of Morocco from 1672 to 1727, often gave the ladies of the court a special present – one of his plops. How generous can you get?

Premium Poo

One particular jobbie has been insured for a great deal of money. It is nine inches long and was found by archaeologists beneath a branch of Lloyds Bank. The reason for its value is that it was passed by a Viking a thousand years ago.

Master Of The (Loo) Rolls

The English king Henry VIII had a servant whose job it was to wipe the royal backside after his majesty had been to the toilet.

Squeamish Sumos

Trainee sumo wrestlers are given the job of wiping the bums of the senior wrestlers. They do not like this job but it has to be done because the wrestlers are so big they cannot reach their bums themselves.

Keep It Under Wraps

Men with long cloaks and buckets were very useful in London in the eighteenth century. They would keep an eye open for anyone who desperately needed to go to the toilet (there were no public lavatories in those days). For a fee of just half a penny the bucket was offered and the desperate individual could do what he had to do, shielded from the eyes of passers-by by having the cloak wrapped around him.

Coffee Break

Workers in an office in St Joseph, Montana, USA, in 1994 complained about the unusual taste of their morning coffee. No one could understand why it tasted so bad so a video camera was set up to keep watch. They soon discovered the reason – a colleague of theirs was creeping into the room, looking around to make sure no one was watching, and then peeing into the pot!

He was of course fired and the video evidence has since been seen on television programmes all over the world.

A Waste of Drapes

In 1712 Ernst August, the Elector of Hanover, recorded that the Russian tsarevitch (eldest son of the tsar) Alexi, son of Peter the Great, pooed in the bedroom and then used the curtains to wipe his bum.

Worth A Billion

The American billionaire Howard Hughes, who died in 1976, kept all his wee in containers. Each container was recorded and labelled. At least it's more original than collecting stamps as a hobby!

Lavatorial Lama

It was once believed that the wee of the Grand Lama of Tibet could prevent disease, so his monks used to mix it in their food.

Tibetan monks also believed that the poo of their leader was holy, so they used to wear bits of it around their necks.

What A Performance!

Ferdinand I, who was king of Naples from 1423 to 1494, had problems with constipation. This made life rather a strain for him so he insisted on having people around him while he tried to empty his bowels. The audience knew he had been successful by the strong smell and sometimes he would proudly show off the poo he had produced.

Fibre Would Be Better

The ancient Egyptians used to put ox bile up their bottoms once a month to clean out their pipes!

Rock Bottom Cheek

At the church of St Helens in Brant Broughton, near Grantham, England, there is a rather rude gargoyle. The fourteenth-century figure is of a man who has lifted his shirt to have a poo. But it proves to be a rather wet poo for the gargoyle dispenses rainwater over the porch of the church.

The Seat Of An Itch

When she got married in 1974, the appropriately named Annie Ramsbottom developed an uncomfortable itch on her bottom. It got worse and worse, and when it developed into a rash she went to see her doctor. When she returned to her parents' home on Dartmoor, England, for a holiday she got to the bottom of her problem. The toilet in her parents' house had a wooden seat, the one in her new house was plastic, and it turned out that she had been suffering from an irritation called Plastic Seat Scratch. The problem was solved when her husband Ralph replaced the offending toilet seat with a wooden one.

Poo Painting

A big argument broke out in New York in September 1999 when the city mayor, Rudy Giuliani, described a painting by British artist Chris Ofili as "sick stuff". The painting, at a big art show, was of the Virgin Mary. Why did Rudy think it was rude? Because instead of paint the artist had made the picture with elephant dung!

Anal Art . . .

One of the art exhibits showed by artist Piero Manzoni in the 1960s consisted of tins of his own poo.

In 1733 the Irish satirist and novelist, Jonathan Swift, famous for his book *Gulliver's Travels*, wrote a treatise called *Human Ordure*. It was all about excrement.

. . . And Dung Dancing

The Zuni Indians of New Mexico had a dance during which they drank lots of fresh urine. The dance was witnessed by an American army captain, John Bourke, in 1855. When Bourke was invited to take part in a similar dance which featured human poo he politely turned down the offer.

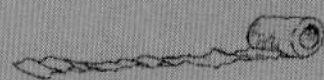

Couldn't Take The Strain

Catherine the Great, the German-born empress of Russia from 1762 to 1796, was suffering with constipation on what turned out to be the last day of her life. She went to the toilet and tried harder and harder to empty her bowels but without success. Eventually she strained too hard and died of heart failure.

The close staff of King George II, who was king of Great Britain and Ireland from 1727, knew that His Royal Highness was a loud and frequent farter and took little notice of the noises from the royal toilet room. But one particularly loud noise in 1760 worried one of his valets. It was a great deal louder than a normal passing of wind. He rushed into the toilet and found the king on the floor. He was dead– he had fallen off the toilet and hit his head against a cabinet.

A Waste Of Money

In the days when it cost only one penny to use a public toilet this little rhyme was often seen written on the walls:

Here I sit, broken-hearted.
Paid a penny
And only farted.

Muck-Spreading Madness

In 1972 Eddie Baker, a farmer in Mytholmroyd near Halifax in Yorkshire, England, collected several hundred gallons of liquid manure from a local chicken farm. As he drove towards his own farm, his muck spreader, towed behind his tractor, suddenly started spraying the foul-smelling (or should that be *fowl*-smelling?) liquid in all directions. All the houses along the

route got a good covering and even the vicar's car, which had the windows open at the time, received its fair share. It was not until a driver hooting his horn drew his attention to the disaster that the farmer knew anything was wrong – and by then 300 yards of road, and everything along it, had been covered in stinking slurry.

Dodgy Draft Dodging

Peter Lenz did not want to go into the West German Army when he received his call-up papers. He reckoned that the only way he could avoid two years in the military was to be turned down on medical grounds. There was just one snag – he was physically fit. And then he devised a solution to his problem. His girlfriend was diabetic, so when he went along for his army medical he took a sample of her urine with him. When he was asked to supply a sample of his urine he swapped it for his girlfriend's sample.

Percy was now confident that he would not be called up but shortly afterwards he received papers saying that he had been passed as completely fit. When he reported to his unit he found out why. "We would have probably believed that you were diabetic," he was told. "But we do not believe that you are expecting a baby!"

Having A Pee

Some people find the statue of the Manneke Pis in Brussels a bit naughty because it shows a little boy having a good long pee. But the statue actually commemorates the story of a little boy who got lost in the city. The father promised that if the boy was found he would erect a bronze statue of the *manneke* (little man). He also promised that the statue would show the boy exactly as he was found. Well, found he was – and he happened to be having a pee at the time so that is what the statue, erected in 1648, shows.

Locked-Up Ladies

Have you heard the popular rhyme about the two old ladies?

Oh dear, what can the matter be?
Two old ladies locked in the lavatory.
They were there from Monday to Saturday
Nobody knew they were there.

In 1982 two French ladies *were* locked in a lavatory for a long period. A burglar who raided their Paris flat made them go into the loo and then jammed the door shut with a couple of chairs. It was not until a relative reported to the police that the old ladies had not been seen for a long time that they were discovered. They had been locked up for nine days, surviving just on water. Luckily, they had plenty of that!

A Very Strange Ceremony

The men of the Chagga tribe in Africa like the women and children to believe that they never poo. When a boy is about to become a man he is taken from his home. He returns home with his bum bleeding and the women are told that his bottom has been plugged and sewn up. From that day forth, the women and children believe that he never farts or does a poo.

When he is an old man he is once again taken away and the operation reversed. After that he can blow off and poo as much as he likes!

In actual fact no operation is ever performed. The boy is initiated into manhood by being repeatedly sat on a bush of thorns. That is the cause of his bleeding. During the ceremony he is ordered never to pass wind, or anything else, where a woman can find out about it. As far as the women and children are concerned he never goes again.

As an old man he is smeared with lamb's blood to let the women and children believe that the operation has been reversed!

It is said that the men's superiority over the women is guaranteed by this strange practice!

CHAPTER EIGHT

Bits and Pieces

This chapter contains stories that did not fit neatly within the other chapter headings in this book. As a result it has ended up as a collection of odd bits and pieces. And, as many of these stories concern torture and punishment, there are plenty of gory human bits and pieces in it as well.

Morning Moons

Every morning in January 1967 an entire platoon of Chinese soldiers would march out, stand with their backs towards the Russian border, and lower their trousers to expose their bare bums. To moon like this is regarded as a great insult and was their way of showing their feelings about Russia. Makes a change from sticking your tongue out at someone you don't like.

The Breeches Maker

In 1555 Pope Paul IV ordered that Michelangelo's paintings be removed from the Sistine Chapel because they showed naked women. This caused a lot of argument and eventually it was agreed that the best solution would be to have clothes painted on them. This job was given to Daniele de Volterra, a pupil of Michelangelo. As a result de Volterra gained the nickname "the breeches maker".

Smelly Flower

The flower *Rafflesia Arnoldi*, named after Sir Thomas Raffles, the founder of Singapore, is very impressive. Its mottled orange-brown and white flower is a metre across. There is only one thing against such a beautiful plant – it stinks like rotting flesh. Because of that it is popularly known as the Stinking Corpse Lily.

I DON'T THINK YOU'VE QUITE GOT THE HANG OF THIS

A Whale Of A Tale

The whaling ship, *Star of the East*, lost two men overboard when trying to harpoon a sperm whale in February 1891. Eventually the rest of the men managed to kill the whale and hauled it aboard, where it was promptly cut up. When they cut into the whale's stomach they received quite a surprise, for there was one of the missing men, James Bartley, alive and well – the whale had swallowed him whole and he had lived to tell the tale!

Anyone Fancy A Stake?

King Vlad ruled Wallachia, now part of Romania, from 1456 to 1462. During that time he is said to have executed over 40,000 people. He gained the nickname Vlad the Impaler because his favourite method of killing was to impale his victims on long stakes.

Vlad was also known as Draculaea, which is Romanian for "son of the Devil". It is thought that Bram Stoker got some of his ideas for the story of Dracula from Vlad's ghoulish activities.

Jump To Your Death, Or Die!

Henri Christophe, the nineteenth-century ruler of Haiti, in the West Indies, wanted to make his country rich and famous but he was extremely cruel in the way he went about it. He demanded absolute loyalty from his men and on one occasion he even ordered a band of them to march over a high cliff to their almost certain death. Those who disobeyed his order were mutilated and killed!

Eventually the people of Haiti (an Indian name meaning "Mountainous Country") rebelled. Christophe's only way out was to commit suicide – he shot himself with a golden bullet.

Bathing In Blood

The Hungarian countess Elizabeth Bathory would drive out of Csejthe Castle in the Carpathian Mountains in the dead of night, in search of young girls. For over six years the countryside was terrorized and numerous unfortunates simply disappeared. The countess had taken them back to her castle, where they were tortured and hung on chains to drain their blood. The countess bathed in this blood, believing that it would preserve her youth and beauty.

Eventually news of Elizabeth's activities reached King Matthias II, who had his men search the castle. They found stores of bodies still hanging in the dungeons.

At the ensuing trial the countess and her men were found guilty of killing some sixty young girls. The men were either beheaded or burned at the stake, but because the countess was of noble birth she escaped this penalty. Instead she was walled up in a room in the castle, her only contact with the outside world being a slit through which scraps of food were passed to her. There she remained for four long years until her eventual death in 1614.

Cross Performance

There have been many weird and wonderful acts performed on stages all over the world. One that proved particularly disgusting to the audience was that of an American performer, Tommy Minnock, in 1934. He planned to finish his act by being crucified. His hands were pierced with nails but then the performance had to be stopped because too many people in the audience had fainted.

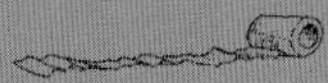

Nails In Nottingham

A man in Nottingham once announced that he would be crucified on Easter Sunday. Each person in the audience was asked to pay £3 to see the nails going into his flesh and 50p to see him hanging on the cross. The performance never took place for it was promptly banned.

Spit Of Danger

French taxi driver Claude Antoine reckoned that he could spit further than anyone else in the world. To do this he had a special technique – he would run across the room on the second storey of a building and then eject his spit out of the window.

In September 1977 he demonstrated his unique technique at a friend's house. Unfortunately he forgot to stop when he reached the window and he fell to the street below. As a result he ended up with two broken legs and a fractured skull.

The Human Ostrich

When Robert Naysmith developed an abscess on his body his doctors opened it and, much to their surprise, found a nail inside. They should not have been too surprised, for Robert had already told them that he earned his living performing as "The Human Ostrich", but they had not believed him. His act consisted of swallowing nails, hatpins, glass, and other highly dangerous (and weird) objects.

As you would imagine, Robert eventually became ill (too much iron in his diet, perhaps?)

He gradually became weaker and weaker and eventually died in April 1906. At the post-mortem the pathologists found over thirty nails and hatpins in his body. Just as well he never walked past an electromagnet: he could have become very attracted to it.

You Can Keepa Your O-Kee-Pa

The Mandan Indians of North America had a pretty gruesome initiation ceremony for their young men. Before a man could be regarded as a real warrior he had first to go without food, drink or sleep for four days. He was then taken into a ceremonial hut where the chief medicine man would use a jagged knife to cut pieces from his chest and shoulders. He would then have wooden skewers pushed through parts of his flesh. As if that were not enough, ropes were then attached to the skewers and the poor man was hung up like a joint of meat. To make the ceremony even more agonizing, weights were attached to his feet and he was spun round until he was unconscious. Then he was handed an axe with which he had to cut off his left little finger, after which he had ropes tied to his wrists and was made to run in a circle until he dropped from exhaustion. He was then regarded as a fully fledged warrior – if he survived!

The ceremony was called *o-kee-pa*, perhaps one of those occasions when it is better to be a wimp than a warrior.

Catch This

The Romanian king, Vlad, known as Vlad the Impaler, whom we have met earlier, was among the first people to use germ warfare. In the 1460s, during his war against the Turks, he gathered a group of people suffering from horrible contagious diseases and sent them into the enemy camp to spread sickness.

Drastic Cure

In olden days it was believed that the ashes from a burned hangman's noose was a cure against evil.

Coming To The Boil

In the reign of King Henry VII of England, boiling was the prescribed punishment for poisoners. According to records at least two people actually suffered this rather warm end.

Fire Power

In England, during Tudor times, burning was the punishment for heresy, and in Scotland it was the punishment for witchcraft. Burning was also used for ordinary women criminals because it was thought to be more "decent" than hanging! Occasionally the victim was strangled as the fire was lit to make death a little less painful.

Just Hanging Around

It was once estimated that 72,000 people were hanged in Britain during the reign of King Henry VIII. It's now believed that this figure is greatly exaggerated, but there were certainly thousands of criminals who met their end in this way, for it was the standard punishment for murder and other serious crimes.

A Punishment To Get Cut Up About

Many people in Britain in the fifteenth to seventeenth centuries were hung, drawn and quartered for even the pettiest of crimes. The condemned man was first hanged but cut down while still alive. Then his body was cut open and his innards drawn out and burned before his eyes. The body was then cut into four pieces. Not a pretty sight.

Rack And Ruin

In the fifteenth century the favoured method of torture in British prisons was the rack. The victim was chained to a table and a system of pulleys stretched his body most painfully. It was nicknamed "The Duke of Exeter's Daughter" because it was introduced into England in 1447 by the Duke of Exeter when he was Constable of the Tower of London. Its use in England was abolished in 1640.

Edmund Campion, a Jesuit jailed for heresy, came off the rack 10 cm (4 inches) taller than before he went on it. Well, it's one way to increase your height!

The Scavenger's Daughter

During the reign of Henry VIII, the Lieutenant of the Tower of London, Sir Leonard Skevington, invented a method of torture called "The

Scavenger's Daughter". Iron bars were placed over the victim's chest and then stamped on until the breastbone broke. Other bars were used to compress the body by bringing the head to the knees until blood was forced from the nose and ears. Charming!

Sometimes it was used for quite unusual crimes, such as that committed by the priest John Bonner. He had apparently committed the unforgivable sin of attracting a larger congregation than the Bishop of London!

A Head (Or Two) For Bowls

The favourite game of the fourteenth-century Mongol conqueror Tamerlane was bowls. Instead of balls he used the skulls of men he had killed in battle.

A Horrid Horn

King Farouk of Egypt, who succeeded his father Faud I in 1936, had a car in which the horn imitated the sound of a dog being run over by the car.

Glass-Bottomed King

King Charles VI of France suffered from bouts of insanity from 1392 up to his death in 1422. He was known as "Charles the Mad" and would not travel in a coach because he believed that his bottom was made of glass and that he might smash it. Presumably he was also frightened of getting a splinter of glass in his bum.

Beany Boots

A driver stopped at a police check in the English town of Colchester, Essex, in 1998 was wearing wellington boots filled with baked beans in tomato sauce. The police never found out why the driver had wellies full of beans but did point out to him that it was an offence not to be in

proper control of a car. No doubt the driver himself was full of beans when the police did not charge him but released him after a warning.

Sick Bag Buff

Many people collect unusual objects but the collection of Ron Sherwin of St Ives, Cornwall, is really sick. He collects airline sick bags (empty ones presumably!).

CHAPTER NINE

The End

"The End" seems an appropriate title for the last chapter in a book, but in this case it refers not to the end of the book but to the end of life. Death is the only certainty in life – it comes to us all in the end. But if you have had a good life there is nothing to be sad about. So let's finish with some funny, some strange, and some weird but true stories concerning our demise.

Strange Companions

In 1830 the twelve-year-old son of Brian Maguire, a famous duellist, died. The father embalmed the boy and carried the body in a glass case wherever he went until his own death five years later.

Ash Cache

In 1991 a Singapore man, Lai Siang Kwong, was fined for keeping 2,000 cremated human remains in his bungalow. He must have had quite a passion for human ash as it was the fourth time he had been caught with a collection of funeral urns.

To Be On The Safe Side

The writer Harriet Martineau was frightened to death of being buried alive. She gave instructions to her doctor that, should she be declared dead, she was to have her head cut off before burial. Well, that's one way of making sure someone is really dead!

Alfred Nobel, the inventor of dynamite and creator of the Nobel Prizes, was also scared of being buried alive. He ruled that all his veins were to be opened and his body cremated. If, as he feared, he had not died that would most certainly have killed him!

Another person with a fear of premature burial was the novelist Edmund Yates. He left a fee of twenty guineas for any surgeon who would slit the jugular vein in his neck before his burial – just to make sure.

Final Flushes

The Roman emperor Heliogabalus was assassinated in a toilet. Whether he had the chance to relieve himself before he was killed is not recorded but no doubt his killer was flushed with success.

The third-century theologian Arius went to the toilet because he was suffering with painful bowels. And there he died.

Henry III, a sixteenth-century king of France, did at least have the chance to go to the toilet before he died. He had just done whatever it was he went in to do and was about to leave the lavatory when he was stabbed to death by a Jacobin friar.

Sleeping In Heavenly Peace

When his wife died in 1959 a Japanese doctor, Karsuaburo Miyamoto, embalmed her body. Then he put her in his bed and he slept next to her every night for the next ten years. Well, at least she didn't snore!

Centre of Attention

When his wife died in January 1775 Martin van Butchell, a London dentist, had her embalmed. With two magnificent glass eyes, and dressed in fine clothing, she was then put on display in his sitting room. It must have been quite a conversation piece when (or perhaps, more likely, if) people came to dinner.

Back To The Land

After battles in the nineteenth century the bones of the dead were often gathered up and shipped back to England. The corpses were not being returned for burial: the bones were ground up and used as fertilizer.

A Fatal Mistake

The funeral of a man who had been poisoned by drinking black market booze took place in the village of Zabaloyte, Ukraine, in June 1988. It turned out to be a fateful day for ten of the mourners. The same illegal drink was served at the funeral wake and they died as a direct result.

William The Exploder

William 1, known as William the Conqueror following his conquest of the British in 1066, died in 1087. Unfortunately his marble coffin proved to be too small. To remedy the situation two soldiers had to stand on the body to push it in. To make the job easier they jumped up and down on the body and broke its spine. The broken spine pierced the stomach and it exploded, splattering the poor soldiers with the remnants of William's last meal. The smell was so putrid that everyone rushed out of the building to get some fresh air.

Cutting Him Down To Size

In the 1840s the Duke of Hamilton paid out an enormous sum of money to buy an ancient Egyptian sarcophagus. It was his wish to be interred in it. But when he died in 1852 he was found to be too tall to fit – so they cut his legs off to get him in.

Crematorium Cremated

The Meadow Lawn Memorial Park in San Antonio, Texas, USA, was once almost cremated itself. This happened when staff had to cremate a body that weighed over 300 pounds. The body burned so fast that they could not control it and part of the crematorium was destroyed by fire as a result.

Going Up In Flames

To burn a human body completely requires a temperature of over 1,650° Centigrade (3,000° Fahrenheit). Do not try this at home.

Fat Is Fast

Fat bodies can be cremated much faster that thin bodies. This is because the fat renders down and adds fuel to the fire.

The Bare Bones

If a dead body is left in the open in warm weather it will take only about nine days for it to decompose and become a skeleton.

Eat Your Words

Emperor Menelik II of Ethiopia believed that he could cure sick people by eating pages from the Bible. It was to prove his downfall. In 1913 he had a stroke and died when he tried to eat the whole of the Book of Kings.

Teeth Of The Führer

When Adolf Hitler, ruler of Germany from 1933, committed suicide in 1945, his teeth, discovered by Russian soldiers, were used to identify his remains. Since then it is believed that those teeth have been locked away somewhere in Moscow.

Concrete Affection

The ashes of the English poet and author D.H. Lawrence, who died in 1930, were taken by his girlfriend Frieda. She had them mixed in concrete, which she used to build a new mantelpiece.

Have A Heart

Marguerite de Valois, wife of Henry IV of France, had pockets attached to the hoop of her dress. Each pocket carried a box in which was the embalmed heart of one of her dead lovers.

She Snuffed It

When Margaret Thompson died in 1776 she left instructions that she was to be buried in snuff. She also decreed that the six greatest snuff takers of the parish should carry her coffin and that they should each wear a snuff-coloured beaver hat. Six young maidens, each carrying a box full of snuff, carried the cloth to cover the coffin and her servant walked in front of the funeral procession spreading large handfuls of snuff on the ground and the watching crowd.

Chocolate For The Worms

The funeral of Roland Ohisson in October 1973 must have been quite a treat for the worms when he was buried. Ohisson, from Falkenberg, Sweden, was a confectionery salesman, so he had his coffin made from chocolate.

A Casket For Antoine

Antoine was one of the top hairdressers of Europe, with royalty among his clientele. But from 1966 he slept every night in a glass coffin made for him by a company in Paris. He believed that it gave him protection from cosmic rays but he also wanted to get used to the idea of dying. He did this because a fortune-teller had told him he would die in the summer of 1976. And the prediction proved to be correct for that is exactly when he did die.

If At First You Don't Succeed . . .

In 1986 an eighteen-stone man tried to commit suicide by hanging himself from an aqueduct over the River Ouse. But he was too heavy and the rope broke. He fell into the river below and drowned.

Performances After Death

The body of John Wilkes Booth, the man who assassinated the American president Abraham Lincoln in 1865, became a great circus attraction after his death. His body was embalmed and sold to a circus which invited local undertakers in the places it visited to inspect it and certify that it really was human, and not a wax dummy!

On one occasion the body was kidnapped and the circus had to pay a ransom to get it back! In life Booth had been an actor but he was seen by more people after his death than ever watched his performances when he was alive!

The Petrified Man

Anderson McCrew, a one-legged tramp, made more money after he died than he ever did while alive. He was killed in a train crash in Texas in 1913 and a local undertaker embalmed his body in the expectation that a relative would claim it and pay the bill. No one ever did claim the body so the undertaker hired the corpse out to a travelling circus.

Billed as the Petrified Man or the Eighth Wonder of the World, the body was exhibited all over America. Eventually the circus went bankrupt and Andy was sold to a woman who kept him in her cellar! He was finally buried in 1973, sixty years after his death!

The Teeth, The Teeth, And Nothing But The Teeth

When a widow saw the ashes of her dear departed husband she knew immediately that they were not his. In the urn with the ashes was

a pair of gleaming false teeth. Her husband had never had false teeth.

Holiday Of A Lifetime

Abraham Finch, a Russian who had settled in America, always longed for a holiday on the French and Italian Rivieras. Eventually, late in life, he had enough money to go with his wife and all the arrangements were made.

Unfortunately Abraham died shortly before departure but his wife decided that he would still have his holiday. She had his body embalmed and took it with her on the boat to Europe. After three months touring France and Italy with her husband's corpse she returned to America, where he was eventually buried.

Giving The Duke His Head

James Scott, Duke of Monmouth, was the illegitimate son of King Charles II, who was exiled from Britain by Oliver Cromwell. In 1685 the duke tried to claim the British throne but was defeated at the Battle of Sedgemoor,

captured, and executed. After the duke had been beheaded it was suddenly decided that there ought to be an official portrait of him. His head was hurriedly stitched back on to his body so he could then pose for the artist. It must have been the only time that the artist did not have to ask his sitter to keep still!

Some Famous Ghouls

One of the favourite activities of the French actress Sarah Bernhardt was to visit the Paris morgue to look at the bodies of the vagrants who had been dragged from the River Seine.

She was so obsessed with death that as a teenager she persuaded her mother to buy her a rosewood coffin lined with white satin. During her life she often slept in that coffin, and when she died in 1923 she was buried in it.

The singer Elvis Presley often spent time at

night visiting the morgue in Memphis, Tennessee, USA, because he liked to look at the corpses.

Famous Last Words

The last words of the English novelist Arnold Bennett were, "Of course the water's safe to drink" as he took a swig of it in Paris. As a result he caught typhoid and died.

Under The Sink

The new tenants of an apartment in Hamden, Connecticut, USA, were very pleased with the premises until they made a gory find beneath the sink – two severed human arms. Luckily it was known that the previous tenant was a Mr Rodrique.

It turned out that Mr Rodrique had an explanation for the arms. He was an orthopaedic surgeon at the Yale School of Medicine and, as he did not have enough free time at work, he brought samples home with him to study. In the hurry to pack up and move he had forgotten all about the arms under the sink!

Hand In Glove

A similar incident occurred in Texas in 1996. A mechanic working on a car opened the glove compartment to discover an amputated human hand. He called the police, who thought they had a murder on their hands. When they questioned the car owner, Alison Hastings, she explained that she kept it in memory of her grandfather, a professor of anatomy.

Meals For A Stuffed Shirt

Jeremy Bentham often attends dinners at University College, London. Nothing remarkable in that you may think, until you discover that Jeremy Bentham died in 1832.

He stated that his body should be used for medical research, so it was dissected at the Webb Street School of Anatomy and Medicine by his old friend Dr Southwood Smith. The skeleton was later reassembled, padded with cotton wool, hay, wood and paper ribbon, and dressed. And to this day Jeremy Bentham resides in a glass case at the university. The head on the body is not actually real – it is made of wax. The real, mummified, head is kept in an oak chest nearby.

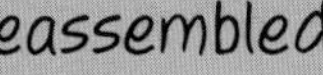

Head Cases

After the English adventurer Sir Walter Raleigh was executed in 1618 his widow carried his head around with her wherever she went. She continued this bizarre practice right up to her death twenty-nine years later. But that was not the end of Raleigh's head because her son, Carew, then took the head everywhere. When Carew died in 1666 his father's head was buried with him.

He Who Lives By The Sword . . .

The Dutch sword swallower Mirin Dajo had a most incredible finish to his act. He would thrust a sword right through his body. Sometimes he would push it through front to back and sometimes sideways. He would then walk into the audience so everyone could see there was no trickery involved – the sword really did go right through his body. In spite of the fact that many in his audience fainted at the sight he repeated this strange demonstration some 500 times during his life. He was even X-rayed to prove that the sword really did go right through his body!

Mirin Dajo continued performing until his adopted country of Switzerland banned his shows. It was, after all, not the sort of thing they wanted other people to try, even if it was a trick. Although banned from public demonstrations he continued to practise his sword swallowing until May 1948, when he died after accidentally cutting his throat – from the inside!